Dearit &
Sharing sunshine
today tomorrow & every

With Love
Gran x.

belifehappy

give. play. love. learn

today. tomorrow. everyday.

Emma Lannigan

BALBOA
PRESS

A DIVISION OF HAY HOUSE

Balboa Press books may be ordered through booksellers or by contacting:

Balboa Press
A Division of Hay House
1663 Liberty Drive
Bloomington, IN 47403
www.balboapress.com
1 (877) 407-4847

Printed in the United States of America.

ISBN: 978-1-5043-2691-9 (sc)
ISBN: 978-1-5043-2693-3 (hc)
ISBN: 978-1-5043-2692-6 (e)

Library of Congress Control Number: 2015901174

Balboa Press rev. date: 02/03/2015

This book was written in response to the challenge a death presented to me. Therefore, *belifehappy* is dedicated to living.

A journey of a thousand miles begins with a single step.
– Lao-tzu, Chinese philosopher (604 BC to 531 BC)

Contents

· ·

Preface

∙ ∙

Reading today, you join the mission of the green butterfly that was created in my mind in April 2008. It is a personal mission to share happiness, of which I'd not realised I had already been on for some time. This book is designed to be there for when you want it. You can open it to any page and know you are the words in your world, and these words are here to offer inspiration, support, and guidance through your journey. They are to offer extra light to your day, so you can share your light by passing the green butterfly on to others.

Before you go on enjoying the words and sharing a dance, song, and love and magic into your world, I'd like to share a little something with you that was shared with me.

It was the beginning of the summer of 2008, and I'd been in my new marketing position for a month. Life was so very different back in the UK, back in a world I thought I'd left behind … or was it that I ran away? The truth is, in that very moment, I was drinking a cup of tea from a very old china cup, and I held the saucer in my hand – very carefully.

My granny, who had just turned a hundred years old that May, was offering me her ear as I talked about life and life without Dad. It had been five months since he had suddenly died, and I was figuring out life. In another life of mine, I would not have believed what happened in Granny's flat on this day – and I wonder whether you will now.

In this moment, I raised my eyes from the china cup and across to meet my Granny's loving, kind smile. As my eyes caught hers, radiant white light streamed from her eyes to mine. There, I felt complete, unconditional love. This was life.

Through pain and loss, I have a lot to be thankful for, and for this reason, I am sharing a poem I wrote for my grandmother who passed away peacefully after 105 years of life.

My only wish is to share the importance of these words with love. x

Giving Thanks

I would like to give thanks for the sparkle in her eye,
I would like to give thanks for the sunshine smiles all the while,
I would like to give thanks for the love in her heart,
I would like to give thanks for where this journey starts.

Birth, life, death,
So the cycle goes.

The journey, destinations, nobody knows,
With joy in our smile and love in our heart,
Walking with purpose, means we are never a part.

Birth, life, death,
So the cycle goes.

We have a choice to be kind,
We have a choice to love,
We have a choice to always know those above,
Stay in our hearts, sharing their love,
Holding our hands when the going gets tough.

Birth, life, death,
So the cycle goes.

It's now a celebration of what we have learned,
It's now a celebration of the love we share,
It's now a celebration of how much we care.

Birth, life, death,
So the cycle goes.

With very much love and thanks.

Acknowledgements

With so many friends and family to thank for supporting me on this writing journey and on the spiritual journey itself, I'd like to start with my sister, Caroline: Thank you for all your listening, supportive hugs, and encouragement. To my mum for being a great mirror and sounding board and for the greater love and understanding it has given us. To my dear friends Gill and Libby, whilst in Cyprus listening to my endless "*belifehappy* is going to be a book!" To a magical and inspirational friend Victoria Whitney, who is probably as passionate about *belifehappy* as I am!

Thanks to the countless wonderfully inspiring mentors, trainers, and other individuals who I met as I trained during 2008 and 2009 during my reiki, holistic massage, and NLP journeys. To Kirsty McKinnon, Victoria Whitney, Alun Jones, Callie Carling, Ed McCosh, Jeff Weigh, and the other wonderful people who supported and contributed to *belifehappy* during 2009 and 2011 with specialist blogs. To everyone who at some point has had a cup of tea with me, sat next to me on a plane, and met me at networking events or through social media – thank you for listening and for your support.

Further thanks goes to the Stamford, Lincolnshire, branch of Cruse Bereavement that supported me in July 2008. Special thanks also to the Events team at the Mental Health Foundation.

I would like to add another special thanks to all the people who have challenged me about belifehappy and to a gentleman who probably kept my determination going as he asked, "how on earth would belifehappy become a global brand?"

This leaves me to thank three more very special individuals. My husband, Steve: Goodness how you have coped with my tears and frustration in believing this book would become a reality, to my wonderment and excitement! Your endless love, belief, and support is felt every day. To my granny, your lifetime is one of my greatest learnings. I finally got to understand your love, kindness, and compassion, for which I am eternally grateful. Finally, to my dad, your gift to me was your death. Somehow, it still doesn't feel a fair trade, and yet together, through your inspiration and my tip-tapping, we are sharing possibly one of life's greatest joys: love.

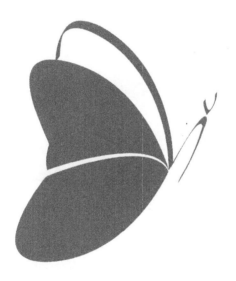

Introduction

. . . .

During a dream in April 2008, tucked cosily under my thirteen-point-five-tog duvet, I was visited by eighty butterflies dancing together above my head. It was calming, peaceful, and a little bit magical, and I knew life was changing.

The following night, I had the same dream. This time, while I watched the eighty dancing butterflies above my head, I watched as another butterfly on its own flew over to join the others: Eight plus one equals nine. The numbers were symbolism of end, completion, and a new beginning. I just didn't know what any of it meant.

This is my belifehappy story—one about a dream, a reality, a life, and a love. Through the beginning of a new journey, these quotes have been written to simply share with you now, right now, today, tomorrow, every day, that we can be life happy.

More than twelve years ago, I found myself in a very dark spiral hole and really could not see life and me together. I was diagnosed with depression, and with support from my GP, family, and close friends, I worked through the darkness and regained my health and some spirit.

What this experience gave me was an opportunity to change and be who I wanted to be. Honestly, I don't think I realised the full extent of the opportunity or embraced the changes as I could.

In 2008, the full stop came to all I had been doing to myself. Life was about to change, and I somehow knew it was. I just didn't know how.

It was a regular Sunday morning while visiting family in the UK, and the next moment, I was in an ICU with my sister and other family as my dad left this world. That was it. During those eleven hours I sat with my unconscious father, I was given an opportunity to embrace change and do it my way: a positive, optimistic way. The key thing from this experience was that it was all down to me. No one in my world could change anything. This time, the whole responsibility was on me.

I transformed my world, values, and beliefs by:

- Learning to love myself for me and to experience true love with my world.
- Learning that simply giving was not enough. If I really loved myself, I would also be open to receiving.
- Learning that it was okay to play and do all the things I loved, which helped me relax, be happy, and be me.
- Learning that my thirst for learning was okay. Actually, there were lots of people out there who also liked what I did. The more I learned, the more people and dear new friends I met.

I have been writing since I was very young. It was in 2005 when I moved to Cyprus that I started to understand that I could actually put a story together. In 2007, I wrote *Finding Happiness*. What I didn't know was that this was the start of my story. Returning to the UK to retrain in holistic therapies and NLP and then choosing to go back to Cyprus in 2009 was confusing for many. What is clear to me was what I achieved while I was there. This book is my complete healing journey. Why did I leave in January 2011? The book was finished, my story was healed, and it was time for action: to start those small steps in my new life with new thoughts and new perspectives.

With my sincerest love, I wish to share with all of you reading this who have or know someone or are experiencing depression, anxiety, panic attacks, IBS, and all manner stress-related illnesses and for those of you who are curious about optimism and challenging your own thoughts and actions. This book is the first positive step forward and is a chance to be honest with yourself and to live the life of your dreams. It's a chance to believe that you will always be supported and loved by the universe. It's your focus towards improving your life without expecting others to change it. You will start to live and love life.

Thank you all dearly for your support, and I do hope you continue to enjoy the energy from the belifehappy butterfly today, tomorrow, and every day.

Emma x

PART ONE

Finding Happiness

25 March 2007

To find happiness, I realised I needed to understand what it is. Happiness has so many meanings, and it means different things to different people. I needed to find out what makes me happy. And if I found that difficult, I would also try to find out what wasn't making me happy.

What I did know was that love would not give me happiness. When I found happiness, I would find love.

On this day, I felt the most amazing experience in my lifetime. It was a feeling of true freedom and spiritual connection that made me smile. A true smile. I was on my own walking on the coast. The sun was warm against a cold wind, the sea an aqua blue reflecting light. I was surrounded by peace and the earth's natural state. Everything was moving at different rates with me in the middle of it all. I was the centre of peace.

The feeling of freedom and relaxation make me happy. Being respected makes me feel happy. Fighting everyday battles at work and home does not bring happiness, but rather is part of everyday life. It is what we do for ourselves that makes the everyday battles easier to deal with.

So does this mean I need to find happiness in my life? The answer is yes, and my journey starts here.

I have tried visiting a clairvoyant, I have read the Kabbalian, I had my first full-body massage, I revamped my hair, I manicured my nails, I walked along the beach, and I updated my CV to push myself forward in my career, all in the last month. Next month, I have an appointment with my UK channellist.

I'm tense and tired. I have spent a day out with a friend watching a rugby match, having Chinese, and watching a funny movie. I'm still tense and tired.

So what is it I want? What should I really be doing? Analysing your life on your own is no easy task. Helping and advising your friends is easy; we all do it. But turn that mirror to reflect your face. Look directly into the mirror, and what do you see? I did this last night, and it frightened me. I was unhappy-looking with a poor complexion and soulless eyes with no sparkle to be seen.

It's not sad. It's just a true reflection of what the continued battles of everyday life have done to me, and action is required. You cannot blame anyone else, and you can't expect anyone else to solve or fix your anxieties. It's your world, and you have to make it what you want.

My realistic aims in life are to be happy (when I discover what that is) and to have a job I enjoy in an environment I am happy in. I want to make the most of my interests and push myself wherever I see an opportunity. As for money, I want to earn money that reflects what I do. Eventually, I would like to own my own house and have minimal debt.

British summertime commenced this week, and the clocks move forward one hour today, 25 March 2007. I have nine months before the end of the year to achieve another piece of the puzzle, but my main priority is to go on the trail of finding happiness that lasts. It will not be easy, and I'm sure I can't go online and print a treasure map that leads me to happiness. It's going to be something that takes my own personal thoughts and experiences, and I have many to look forward to.

Eleven months later ...

PART TWO

Steak, Mashed Potatoes, and Onion Gravy

Saturday, 9 February 2008

I haven't slept. I walked through Mum's door at eight-thirty this morning, feeling very tired after my journey from Paphos to Gatwick last night. It had been a normal day at work, just tidying up a few things before I had a week's holiday back in the UK. I'd badly needed this holiday after the few months I'd had.

Last summer, I had worked very crazy hours organising and working on a television programme that aired in January and continued into February. I'd also been going out with "him" for the third time, and this time, things had been much better, even spending some time with his parents. In October, I had had to fly back to the UK to work on the postproduction of the programme in Manchester and decided to have an additional week's holiday to see my dad and sister. Whilst I'd been working on the filming, Caroline had called to tell me Dad was in a bad way financially and that he was considering declaring bankruptcy. Leaving it with me to think of a plan, I decided to take a loan out myself to pay off the biggest of Dad's debts. So the trip in October was about going to the bank with him to pay it off. A relief for us all, but it wasn't the end or the answer to his many problems. At the end of that trip and returning back home to Cyprus, the "him" sent me a text (as was his usual fashion) to say he could no longer see me and wouldn't be collecting me from the airport. I guessed I wouldn't be having the Sunday lunch he'd promised either.

During December, my close colleague was having to travel back to the UK as his father was losing a years-long battle with cancer. It was coming to the end of the holiday year, and I had a lot left, but on each application, I had to cancel as my colleague was called away. The Christmas party was hell (at first), with the ex parading his new girlfriend around. As he said, "it was all about the perception I chose." The night turned in my favour, winning the final award of the evening for all my work on the rebranding of the company (which no longer exists). I came back to the UK for Christmas.

My granny was ninety-nine, and as with every Christmas, we didn't know if it would be her last. The whole family was there for dinner. On Christmas Eve, Dad came down from Derby, and we went to the local pub with Caroline to have a few drinks in the afternoon with friends. If I hadn't had enough of exes, here was another and his partner. The two of them sat happily next to me and chatted with my dad for most of the afternoon. Dad seemed okay, but his leg was hurting, and having to go outside to smoke his pipe was a pain. Caroline decided we would have Chinese takeout for tea. I remember feeling happy because Dad, my sister, brother in law and I could have this time for us. I was leaving on Boxing Day morning to fly back to Cyprus and just wanted to spend time with Dad. But no, for some reason, the ex and his girlfriend were invited, too. It was awful. I paid for Dad's takeout, ate, and left by nine. At eleven-thirty on Christmas Day night, I said my goodbyes, and my brother in law drove me back to Mum's. I hugged my dad, feeling his burnt orange wool jumper on my face and smelling his pipe tobacco. His arms felt weaker around me. How was I ever to know?

But good news followed, and I met a wonderful man in a bar in Paphos just before New Year's Eve. I'd been dreading New Year's, spending the last two with "him" and friends, and this year, there wasn't an invite for me. This extremely tall man saved me and only turned out to be my "gift from the universe." Three days prior, I received a phone call from him in the middle of the night. He was in Norway, and I was in Cyprus. He declared his love for me and asked me to pack up all my things and come live with him. Wow, now that's news. Yesterday morning, he'd emailed saying maybe he had been a bit hasty and that we'd see how things went. I knew I wanted to stay in contact with him. Alcohol talks a different language, sober or not, I have no idea which talks the real truth!

I arrived in Gatwick at twelve-thirty this morning. I decided to travel back to Peterborough via the train, and this meant I had to wait in Gatwick for the trains to start running. Straight out of the baggage area and through customs, I headed for Costa Coffee, had a large cup of tea, and then headed outside for a cigarette. It was cold. I had to find somewhere to sit to try to get some sleep. I found that place. It was exciting and probably the scariest thing I have done or felt, and I will never do it again. I found the place that you see on television in the news where the hardcore travellers sleep. I was about to become one. I walked around a corner and found about a hundred people, all asleep on those very uncomfortable-looking rows of seats. Some people were upright with their shoes off and feet on a coffee table. Others had coats, blankets, or even sleeping bags over them, and all had a rucksack or coat under their heads as a pillow. It was silent all but for the flooring-cleaning machine whirring around us. I'd spotted three available seats and sat down. I was nervous to sleep in case someone took my bag or something worse. After about ten minutes, I was just too tired, so I set my alarm on my mobile phone for four in the morning, giving me at least three hours of sleep. I put my phone on silent with the alarm on vibrate so not to wake or disturb the other travellers, took off my trainers, and placed them under the seat. I placed my suitcase upright in front of where my head lay on my rucksack and placed my aeroplane blanket over me. Rest. At two-forty-five, my phone buzzed under my ear. The extremely tall man had texted me. He said he loved me.

So, I'd had no sleep, but I felt pretty good someone loves me. The plan for today was to do not very much, and I would meet up with my sister then go to bed early so I could catch up on the sleep I've missed.

Sunday, 10 February 2008

Dad called me yesterday morning around eleven. Mum was out, and the phone rang. My friends don't call me here, but I answered. It was Dad. He'd just spoken to my sister to check that I was back. We talked about me being tired from the journey. In fact, if I'm honest, I moaned about it. He sounded okay, but a bit down. The reason I'm back is on 29 December, as I lay in bed sleeping, my mobile rang. It was my sister and early in the morning, too. Dad was in hospital (at which my heart started pounding). He had fallen at home and broken his femur of his leg which was amputated below the knee. He was having an operation to have a pin placed. I asked if I should come back, but she said no and that she would keep in touch. I was awake now, and the reality was my dad had just had more bad luck.

Dad and I spoke about what he was up to, and I said I would come and visit on Monday, as well as Wednesday, as arranged with my sister. He said I shouldn't worry because of the cost of the extra train fare. I told him not to be silly and asked if he had had chance to read the paperwork we'd sent about moving to be nearer to family again.

"No I haven't."

"Well do you think you could before Wednesday? Caroline went to a lot of trouble to get the paperwork."

"Yes OK."

"So what are you doing today?" I asked.

His friends have sixteen friends and family members staying, and they were having a meal. He said he'd been invited round but didn't think he'd go. "I can't get out of the flat with the wheelchair and I need someone to get me and bring me back."

"Well I'm sure they won't mind, just pop round for a bit and get some company. I'll be up on Monday and we can catch up."

I left the conversation that I would call in the morning and confirm when I would be arriving. I'd been thinking today how nice it would be if I get off at Alfreton and pop to the supermarket and get Dad and I steak. I'd make us steak, mashed potatoes, and onion gravy in the flat and then just watch some TV together, just like we used to when we lived together, back when I was twenty-two.

The phone rang at ten-twenty-five; Mum had answered it. Her face changed, and I knew something was wrong. I knew before I booked and paid for my flight over here that this trip would not be a good one. Mum put down the phone.

"Who was it?" I asked in my I'm-not-happy voice. I knew I wouldn't like the news, so I was preparing myself for the worst.

"Caroline. Your Dad is in an ambulance. They're trying to sort him out."

I went upstairs. It was planned today that I would go out for Sunday dinner with Mum, my Step-father, and my granny and then meet up with some of my old school friends. I'd already dressed in my skinny jeans, my long blue top, and a cream crocheted jumper with the brown pashmina scarf Lidia had given me from her trip to Egypt. I had my makeup on and my hair all done.

I grabbed my rucksack, emptying it of all my flight items, and packed a pair of jeans, two tops, and two pairs of knickers and socks. I grabbed my toothbrush and toothpaste, makeup bag, and hairbrush.

I went downstairs and did what I do best at any time of crisis or stress: I had a cigarette outside. When I got in the kitchen, my mum was stood there.

"I just can't think what they mean by sorting him out – are they keeping him alive?" I asked

"I know, that has crossed my mind," she replied.

I went outside and lit another cigarette. Panic and my heartbeat were all raising within me. Dad had been poorly many times. He had been diagnosed with diabetes when he was thirty-eight years old. I was eight years old then.

The doorbell rang, and my sister appeared sobbing and hysterically trying to get her words out. "We've ... got ... to ... go ... Emma. It's ... really ... serious ... this ... time."

"My bag is packed." My sister panicked openly in a crisis, and I always remained calm on the outside. She had filled her car with petrol on her way over with the intention to drive up. She was leaving my nephew with mum, but she couldn't take the car. She was panicking that we might never make it ourselves, and as they had one car, my brother in law would need it for my nephew.

I got her to see reason, and her husband also said he did not want her driving, so we drove back to her house. Mum had called a taxi to pick us up and drive us to Peterborough train station. We knew what time the train was as Caroline had taken this journey a few weeks ago with my nephew to visit Dad in hospital when he had broken his leg.

Caroline rushed in the house and grabbed her toothbrush. She was also diabetic; she and my dad were both were Type 1 insulin-dependent. I reminded her to get her insulin and her bedtime injection too as we may need to stay overnight. Yes, she would need a coat. We both popped to the toilet, and I realised I had started my period, and I had only one tampon in my bag. Caroline rushed to get me pads and tampons. After maybe two or three rushed cigarettes on the drive, the taxi arrived.

Both very apprehensive and anxious, we got in the taxi and put on our seatbelts. We didn't speak for most of the twenty-minute journey, and we both knew the driver sensed our urgency to get there. At the station, I went into organised mode and sent Caroline off to get sandwiches, crisps, a drink each, and some chocolate. I went to get the tickets. I knew singles would be okay.

The train arrived, and we found seats opposite a woman engrossed in her magazines. For that moment, I wished I were her. We had an hour until Nottingham. After a change for Derby, we should arrive by one-thirty. Dad was taken in at ten-thirty that morning. Caroline needed to have lunch, so she could have her insulin. Neither of us felt like a mouthful of food, but we ate. Caroline's mobile rang. It was Dad's friend. Tears were falling down Caroline's face, and I took a deep breath. She said she'd had tried to call the hospital, but the hospital wouldn't tell her anything and that she had told them we were on our way. She also mentioned a name of something they thought Dad had. We called Mum. I spoke to her as she was in the middle of her Sunday lunch and it didn't sound like she wanted to be interrupted; that was just her way. I got off the phone quickly before she upset me. We ate our lunch. About twenty minutes before our change at Nottingham, we received a second call from Dad's friend.

Dad was in intensive care, and we should try to get there as soon as possible. Panic. We agreed was to get off at Nottingham and get a taxi to take us directly to Derbyshire Royal Infirmary. I asked Caroline to try to be calm; we just needed to get there.

In amongst all these feelings, the rational and reality of things still takes place. Caroline did not have much cash on her. I had cash and a credit card, so I would just pay for everything and we would sort it out later. There was no time to worry about money.

We stopped and had a cigarette. You think they help calm you, but they really don't. In the taxi, we set off. Staring out of the window of the black cab, I watched as Nottingham went about its Sunday business. Caroline had to direct the driver to the entrance of the hospital. We arrived by one. We had a cigarette, and it was okay as I had bought 400 duty-free and packed four packets in my rucksack. We wouldn't run out.

We knew this hospital very well. In 2002, we spent every weekend here visiting Dad for six months while they tried to save his infected leg. After six months of morphine and various drugs, they amputated his right leg below his knee. But we hadn't been to intensive care, and I'd joked that this time, Dad had been promoted as such to this ward. It wasn't funny, though. Not one bit.

We decided to go in through the main entrance and then walk the very long route past our usual side entrance past junction eleven (where the toilets are). We turned right to the lift to intensive care. I just felt sick and anxious to see Dad. I figured it'd be okay; they'd get his levels (sugar) stable, and he'd be out in no time. I'd never been in an intensive care unit before we walked looking at every bit of information on the boards and signs. There was a call button, and Caroline pressed it. In any intense situation, Caroline does everything; she's older. I just help make all the decisions, but Caroline does it. We were asked to wait in a side waiting room until a doctor could come and see us. Our phones switched off. We entered this square room with that institutionalised pink paint on the walls. It was hot, so we took off our coats and placed our bags on the floor. We were here and just wanted to see Dad.

There was another lady next to Caroline. Some of her family arrived. It had been more than twenty minutes, so I went out to see if we could find anything out. On the wall was a leaflet about ICUs, and in one paragraph, I felt a small ounce of joy that we could ring the bell again. So I did. They would be out in a minute. Caroline and I then began a ritual that would last for nine hours of pressing down the antiseptic hand soap before entering the unit. A woman opened the doors and ushered us into a side room much smaller than the one before. She said she just had to attend to something and would be back in a moment.

A young woman in her thirties with blonde mousey-coloured hair partially tied back in a ponytail sat near the door. I was by the wall, and Caroline facing her. This was it.

"Your Dad is very poorly, when he was brought in this morning he had a cardiac arrest in the ambulance. They brought him into A and E where he had another cardiac arrest, which took six minutes to revive him. They then transferred him to ICU. There are many complications, and I need to make you aware of how seriously ill you Dad is before you see him."

At this point, I decided to say, "I'd better sit next to Caroline now as I think she will need me." I moved to the seat next to Caroline, and we held hands.

"Your Dad has very high blood sugar levels which we are trying to stabilise. There are other complications that in his left leg his pulse has stopped and there is no blood circulating. His hormone gland in his stomach (which controls all the hormones in your body) has ceased functioning. We are monitoring him and he is on several medications to reduce his blood sugar and to increase his blood pressure. Until we do this we are unsure of the actual cause of his illness. Now, he is currently on a ventilator to give his lungs a rest...."

I interrupted; "He's not breathing for himself? Well, that's not good ... he can't breathe for himself." Squeezing Caroline's hand harder, now very scared, and now ironic as I actually needed her at that moment.

"No."

You no longer become yourself as I screamed the sound of only pain and sobbed. We both sobbed and held each other.

"Can we speak to him?" I asked.

"No, I'm afraid he's unconscious. He's in what we call a reverse coma. Which causes severe brain damage."

"So we can't talk to him?" A long silence. With desperation, I asked, "will we ever be able to speak to him?"

"I'm afraid it is very unlikely that your dad will recover. The extent of the damage that has been caused during this had made his body very weak."

At this moment, I knew that was it. My dad was not coming out of here alive. But you have to have some hope.

The doctor asked, "Has your Dad been depressed recently?" We both said that he had. He had been stuck in a wheelchair for six weeks and not able to get about in the flat, let alone outside. I thought nothing more of it.

The doctor then explained how the unit worked and that we could stand with Dad and use the side room if necessary. If we left the ward, we would have to ring the buzzer to be let back in.

I was scared. I was scared to see my own dad. What if I cried in front of people?

"I can't go in... I don't want to cry in front of people." The doctor explained that in this type of ward staff and patients are aware of the emotions of family and it was absolutely fine and at times they would pull the curtain round to give Dad some privacy.

We walked across to the window where Dad was. There were so many machines and monitors, tubes, and junctions of tubes. In ICU, there is an assigned team of nurses and a doctor to the patient, and there is someone there all the time. It was a real comfort.

Caroline walked over to Dad and stroked his hair off his face and said hi. I said hi, too. It always seems irrational to speak to someone who is unconscious.

"It's OK he will probably hear you, so talk to your Dad so he knows you're here," the nurse told us. We talked, but this was too much. We needed a warm drink and a toilet stop. We also needed to contact our uncles, as we were advised.

Down the lift, we turned right up to junction eleven for the toilet. I went outside to meet Caroline, who was already making calls to her husband and our uncles. I tried to make a call on my mobile; however, as I had a Cyprus SIM card, for some reason, it wouldn't let me. At best, I could send texts and receive calls, so I texted my best friend, Lidia, to tell her my dad was dying. She called me straight away. After two cigarettes, we headed back inside. My uncles would be here in under three hours.

We went up to see Dad and stood by the window as the nurse busied away checking and changing tubes and medication. The nurse asked if we would sign for Dad's personal effects: his watch and the bag he had brought in. He had no money.

The nurse then said, "Oh, there's only one...."

And we both laughed and said, "one shoe!" She realised what she had done. Dad had only one shoe because the other was on his prosthetic leg. What we might not have realised at the time was that we were actually taking Dad's belongings – his jogging bottoms, shirt, watch, and hankie.

Caroline was stood close to Dad's leg when the nurse said, "Oh I'd advise you not to look, as you know the circulation has stopped." I could only guess that it was blue or something. Every time a nurse changed or checked something on Dad, they always said, "Martin I'm just going to check your temperature." Or whatever. Their respect was amazing, and their care for us so warm and familiar. By around five, Dad's friends had arrived. They had been driven over by their daughter. It was uncomfortable, and there were too many mixed emotions. Only two people could be at Dad's side at once, so Caroline and I let them say goodbye. I sat in the side room on a chair opposite Dad's friend. It was then I knew for sure that my Dad was not coming out of here. He'd be gone very soon.

I went outside for another cigarette, and Caroline asked me to call her husband to update him. I explained to him Dad was dying.

About five minutes later, Uncle Jim arrived with Auntie Linda. No more than thirty minutes later, Uncle Brian arrived with Auntie Carol. Dad's friends left as they had a party of sixteen to feed. The family sat in the side room. The doctor came in and updated my uncles. Uncle Brian was a GP, and we all hoped he would understand what was happening to Dad. You could see the pressure we were putting on him, but we needed him. He got up and went over and spoke to the doctor. I could see him at the end of Dad's bed looking at charts. It was after six-thirty. They were concerned for Caroline and me and said we must go and check into a hotel and come back. We didn't want to leave, but we knew we would have nowhere to stay the night.

This wasn't real and couldn't be happening. It was dark now, and we walked across the road towards the train station where we knew there were several hotels. We entered the second and approached the desk. I asked the receptionist about a room, but he pretty much rushed us out as we had not made a reservation. We went into the next hotel. The lady at reception was just as cagey. Goodness, we just needed a room. I mentioned that we had to get back to the hospital, and her mood changed. She must have been able to seen the pain, shock, and exhaustion on our faces. Within a minute, she had found a room for us. I gave her my card details and took the room key. We dropped off our bags and headed straight back, both stopping for a cigarette before entering the hospital grounds.

Back in the side room, the doctor came back in. They were now waiting to see how Dad reacted to the medication. They advised us to go and get something to eat. We could come back and see him, and they would call us or we could call them at any time of the night. Uncle Brian needed to get back as he had surgery tomorrow. Jim and Linda said they would stay with us for something to eat and then head back home.

Caroline and I popped over to see Dad, just letting him know that we were just going to be away for a short while to get some food. At this point, though, Dad had been given a sedative, which meant now he would not be able to hear or sense anything.

We walked across the road, having a cigarette on the way. We went into an Italian right opposite the hospital. Jim and Linda ordered very strong Americanos, Caroline a half a lager, and for me a lemonade. We all ordered lasagne. We talked but not much; we were hungry. Caroline's mobile rang. We had just finished our meal. It was ICU, and we needed to come back in.

We both got up; Uncle Jim said they would follow us over, and they'd sort the bill. We practically ran out of the restaurant while the owner looked at us aghast. We had time for that cigarette before we went in. Up in the lift, antiseptic soap, and the buzzer: We went in. The lights were dimmed on the ward now, and we were taken over to Dad where a curtain had been drawn. He had a heat blanket on him under the heavy white cotton sheet.

Uncle Jim and Auntie Linda arrived. The doctor explained, "We are unable to give your Dad anymore mediation as if we do, it will cause more harm, we are not going to withdraw any medication, but we cannot give him anymore and we will see how he progresses."

The four of us sat by his bedside, the two visitors only rule no longer applied. The night team had been changing over shifts for the last hour, and the doctor and nurse who had been there all day were leaving. The nurse said, "I'm so sorry." It was as if he had already gone.

By eight-fifty, I went outside again. There was nothing I could do, and those machines – there is nothing you can do. I had a cigarette and made my way back in. The nurses had made coffee, and as I walked in, she made me a cup of tea and brought it over. We were so tired. I was so tired. Uncle Jim was aware of the time, and he needed to start driving back as he had to be at work at five the next morning. It got to just before nine-forty-five, and we started to walk out with them. The doctor came over and said he needed to speak to us. We explained we just needed to have five minutes. Uncle Jim and Linda decided to stay with us. As we walked up the tunnel hallway past the junctions, I turned to Linda and said, "Thank you for staying, I really don't think we can do this on our own." She put her arm around me, and we walked up the stairs to the ICU.

All of us sat at Dad's side. Two nurses stood with us; one knelt in front of Caroline and explained what would happen next.

"We have run some more tests and spoken to our consultant and your Dad has not made any progress. Because of all the complications, and we can't get his blood sugar below 50 which is not even a recordable figure and you can see that his blood pressure is very low. For the bodies organs to function the blood pressure needs to be above 75 and your Dad's has been much lower all day. We cannot give your Dad anymore medication as this will cause more harm, and therefore we would like to ask you to withdraw the medication and let your Dad fight on his own." Shock. "Even if your Dad does stabilise I must emphasise the damage and complications he has would mean he would not survive an operation. As you both know, his other leg requires amputation. And when we checked his stomach earlier, an amount of old blood was found. Your father is very ill, and it is your decision to allow him to go peacefully."

We all looked across at each other. This doesn't happen. But it does.

"Ask any questions you like?" the nurse said.

It was like Caroline and Uncle Jim understood and knew the medication had to be stopped. I couldn't, and they knew I wasn't going to agree.

"But I know Dad is very ill, I just don't want him to go." Auntie Linda held me as I sobbed, and I held my dad's hand. My dad was about to die.

"What will happen now is we have stopped all the medication, and I am going to turn the ventilator down. Please don't worry, but I am placing this syringe of morphine here (near a tube in his shoulder) should for any reason your Dad appear to be in pain and I will come over and press down the syringe, which will in itself kill him. We should not need it but it is a precaution for your Dad's comfort. Now I will stand over by the curtain to give you your privacy but will be keeping an eye on the monitors. You will see that you Dad will start to deteriorate quite quickly, however if it does appear to be taking longer I will come over and turn the ventilator down a little more."

Caroline and I knew this was it. Dad could miraculously pull through and stabilize, or he would die. I held his hand and looked to the floor where I saw they had even turned the heat blanket down. He was cold already. I looked at my Dad's face and said in my head, *Dad they have done everything possible to help you today, and now only you can decide to fight or to go. Dad I love you very much and if you choose to go that's OK, but I and we would all very much like you to stay. But I understand. And it's up to you, it's your choice.*

Through tears, we all sat looking at the monitor to see his heart rate and blood pressure reducing. At a sudden moment, I saw Dad swing his head around. He looked at me and then swung back. I shuddered. It wasn't possible; he had tubes all across him. I didn't say anything. We waited, and then from the corner, I saw the nurse move over and turn the ventilator down. My dad was lying there in front of us, and no one could save him. The light in the ceiling dimmed. Caroline, Uncle Jim, and I looked at each other; it flickered and dimmed again. At five minutes past eleven on Sunday night, 10

February 2008, my dad died, and no one knew exactly why, but we all saw the light.

For what seemed a long time, I had sat and held my dad's hand, stroking his thumb with mine. Caroline was touching his arm. When he passed, she got up, stroked his hair, and gave him a kiss. I was scared and numb, but I stood there, kissed the top of his head, and said "Bye Dad. Have a safe journey." My heart was breaking. Linda held me, and Uncle Jim held Caroline. We had to leave; we couldn't do anymore. As we walked towards the exit of the ICU, the nurse came over and said how sorry she was and handed us a booklet on what to do when someone dies in England and Wales. It was the first of many booklets. She asked what we would like to do with Dad's things, and we agreed to collect them the next morning.

Walking down the stairs, everything was different now. We walked down all the junctions to the coffee machine. It was out of order. So we walked towards the main entrance and stopped at another machine. Getting us all a drink, we then walked outside into the night. It was midnight. Caroline made some telephone calls, and I texted Lidia. She called me back. We stood and talked and knew Uncle Jim had to get off, so we said goodbye and walked slowly towards the hotel.

It's not happening. It's not real. This is not happening, and it is not real, I thought.

We walked in and decided to get a drink from the bar – a drink to Dad. Caroline ordered a white wine, and I ordered a Bacardi and coke.

A New Recipe

April 2008

It's April 2008, and it's been three months since I watched my dad pass away, and I've not been long in my new home (my fourteenth in the last twenty-one years). I'm sat at the desk I've set up in my spare room. I'm thinking about what I'm going to do. What is my life going to be about? I've just watched morning news on TV and was amazed at how unhappy and miserable the UK appears to be. This was the reason I left the UK to live abroad three years ago.

My mind heads back to the days of Mr Motivator in the morning, and I think about how the UK can get happy. I'm doodling on my notepad (I do this a lot), and I start to write a series of words. Then came be life happy. It just made sense.

So what next? Fear. You know that feeling of if I don't do what everyone else does, then I won't be successful? I wondered if unhappiness was my life, or if I could choose something else.

A few months earlier, as I packed up my house and prepared to move back to the UK, I needed to sell my car. It was one of the last things holding me up, and I really needed someone to buy it. Kind friends put out the word, and a couple someone knew needed a second car. My car was a little run around, so it was perfect. They agreed to buy it, and the over the next few days, I spent a bit of time with the couple. I was in a new place; my dad had just died; I was thirty-one years old; and I was leaving my job, my friends, and a country I was going to call home. My head was all over the place. Oh, and I'd broken up with a guy I really liked, loved I guess, some months before and kind of still had that around me.

Exhausted one afternoon after packing more boxes and just hanging up from a call with my ex calling to see how I was getting on, I flaked out across my bed. The blinds were down to block out the light, and above my bed was the central room light. I stared up at the ceiling. And in this moment, I heard, "I don't know what you're doing or why you're doing it, but you'll be OK, that's all I can say." And then my Dad's voice left the room, as did the smell of his pipe smoke.

In a different country, the selling of a car had a completely different process, and here in a queue, waiting to do the final sign over of ownership, the couple and I got talking about stuff. The lady said, "You know with the way you think about life Emma, you should read the *Celestine Prophecy*... you sound just like the book." Right then, I thought I'd heard of this book before; however, back then, any suggestions would have flown right by me.

Back in the UK, at my desk, I'm thinking about life. Where is it taking me? Thirty-one, single, and no plans for where to work. What to do?

A few days on, the phone rings. It's my sister, and she tells me there is a job going at a local company for a marketing position that has not been advertised yet. Perfect. I called and sent off my CV. I'd worked in marketing since I left uni, and I love a challenge, so the job sounded perfect. A perfect solution to my fear.

I go off to a bookstore in search of *The Celestine Prophecy* with some kind of urge that it's the right thing for me to do. As I head over to the book stand of mind, body, and spirit, I see a book with angel wings: *How to Hear Your Angels* by Doreen Virtue. Interesting. While I was abroad, one of the PAs once gave me a CD of Doreen Virtue to help me relax (little did I know until eighteen months later that this lady was an earth angel, a reiki master.) I picked the book up knowing, just knowing, I was to buy this book. I searched for *The Celestine Prophecy* and also came across *The Alchemist* (my first introduction to Paulo Coelho.) I was set.

After my A levels, especially English literature, I always remember saying I would not read a book again for a very, very, very long time. (I was also told by an English teacher at school that my English was not good enough to be a writer.)

Back at home, I got settled in my sister's nursing chair. I had no furniture when I moved into my new UK home, and she needed a temporary home for this nursing chair and stool. It's great, so comfy, and the seat and footstool rock together. At my side is a wonderful sideboard, another donation from a friend, which holds my cup of tea. (I love tea.) Warm, comfy, and safe, I opened up the first book, *The Celestine Prophecy*. I was hooked. I get up only to make another cup of tea and smoke a cigarette in the back garden. I want to stop, but I'm just not ready yet.

For two days, my body was comfortably supported in the nursing chair, gently rocking, sometimes stopping for a moment as the words from the page sparked light bulbs. Each time, everything seemingly got brighter. I was hooked.

It's okay, though, I have two more books to read. My mind was now an absolute sponge for all this new information. The covers say these books have sold millions (and we know they have).

Where this is all taking me, I have no idea. What I do know is that it's okay.

I get a letter in the post inviting me to an interview for the marketing job. What a relief. I have a presentation to do, and it looks like a four-hour interview. A new suit is required, and I've not worn one of those for about four years.

Standing in Marks and Spencer's, I see this lovely suit dress. It's cute, it's serious, and it's professional. I try it on, and I feel amazing. I look amazing. (The size twelve body is simply down to a tough six months.) The dress is a size fourteen, although this fact is irrelevant to the job I'm applying for!

The job interview goes very well, and I'm still feeling really good. It's all part of a new phase, and I'm going with it. The phone rings; I have the job starting in June. Job, house to live in, car, suits, money in the bank: I'm sorted. Oh, I'm single, but that's okay right now. (Seriously, it is. Just now!)

With five new suits and a nine-to-five marketing manager position, I'm all go. Forward or backwards?

2008: a new life. Pressing the pause button.

Finding Love

It is fast approaching a time of year that I would once dread. It is fear of the reminder of being single and/or the fear of my partner forgetting. It was once very important to feel loved. With no love inside, it must come from other?

Did I know I had no love? Of course, I loved. The difference was that I wanted it back, and when I didn't get it back, I clearly wasn't loved. Therefore, why should I show love? Are you with me? For what appeared in my world was society (my family, friends and work buddies) had expectations of love and what it should be. I was never one to hug a friend: You know personal space and everything! It was at university when I met an incredible lady who was what we call a friend for a reason (as sadly I have not been able to get in contact for the last couple of years.) She taught me from the age of eighteen about drinking. She also showed me how I could care about people and show affection towards friends. She was my first friend I could openly go up and hug when I met her in the street. She was an inspiring friend.

So for the next ten years, this is what happened. The expectations still were there in my life. I didn't settle down in a relationship until my mid twenties. I was far too busy building a career because I felt it was expected of me. When I did finally settle down, I felt it was the one, and now I sadly looked back and realised it wasn't. I still didn't know what love was. I then went on to make huge changes in my life, still searching. As my ex said in a card as we parted, "I hope you find what you are looking for." Much wiser than me because I had no idea what I was looking for. Was it still love? The move introduced me to another new friend, who is thankfully still very dear and close in my life (When I say *close*, I mean in friendship, not proximity. We don't live in the same country and haven't for a few years.) This lady has a huge heart, and she might remember at first I really didn't know how to relate to her. She cared, she cried (I know I didn't cry for quite a few years!), she loved, she showed so much affection towards people, and it helped them feel good. Not one day in the time we were in the same country went by without her saying, "Emma you look gorgeous today, simply beautiful my babe!" I can tell you now when I had to leave and travel back to the UK that I missed that very much. I did not realise how much joy this lady was showing me. It all came to a stop. Suddenly.

The last time someone told me they loved me romantically was two years ago. Then it was time to learn what love really was.

Still Finding Love

On Sunday, 10 February 2008, my dad died. No one knew exactly why, but we all saw the light. For what seemed a long time, I had sat and held my dad's hand stroking his thumb with mine. Walking down the stairs afterwards, everything was different.

What does death mean for love? This was how I found out what love was. In the events after this sudden loss in my life, I started to ask myself questions. I wanted to know why on earth this had happened to me? Victim? I was queen of the victims, but to me, I had lost my dad and that was all that mattered. When you depend so much on others for your happiness and for their love, when it is gone, you are left empty. It is a fact.

Was happiness a route to love? It was my first question: How do I find happiness? And the answer was I am to find love? Now this wasn't a "get out there Em and find a boyfriend!" The reality was I could not find a boyfriend as I had nothing to offer. I was empty.

I coasted for a while. One afternoon in July, I remember sitting with my granny in her flat. We had a cup of tea, and we were talking about my dad. I found it easy to talk to her about him, and she always listened. Then, while we were talking, I remember saying, "thank you Granny I know I have gone on a bit, I just wanted to talk to someone who understands." Then I saw from that very moment rays of pure unrefined love started streaming from her eyes. I felt all love around me. I know it's not the kind of love I thought was expected; this was unconditional love. It was like a miracle, a gift to me.

I've Found It Over Here: Love

My next stop was a trip to see my dear close friend, and this trip is the one I refer to as the start of my journey, because it was on this trip I made decisions to change my life. I discovered what I was looking for. It took four or five years after my ex wrote, "I hope you find what you are looking for." Within months, I had left my job and started along the reiki healing path. With reiki, I felt a completeness and a channel of the highest intentions. I felt at home.

Five Years Later

25 March 2012

In an email to myself five years later after writing Finding Happiness, I realised just what I had learned and how I now trusted the guidance and inner knowing. At last not only had I found love within myself and trust, I had found happiness too.

From: emmalannigan
Subject: What I have learned
Date: 25 March 2012 23:10:32

Establish what your stuff is.

Tidy your stuff up.

Be ready to walk away from the stuff that is no longer supporting you.

Be focused on what new stuff you're looking to support you.

Be sure you've cleared the old stuff.

Now get on, and when the new stuff comes, you'll be ready.

With no stuff in sight, you're now greatness and light.

belifehappy

PART THREE

Sunny Side Up

belifehappy: Why Not?

8 September 2009

Because why not belifehappy? You have a choice every second, minute, hour, and day. Not yesterday or tomorrow. Today.

Some people choose to be unhappy, as it gives them attention from family, friends, co-workers, and employers. It's not always good attention, but at least it's attention.

You can wake up in the morning, stub your toes, feel a bit fuller because it's that time of the month, see the kids have toothpaste on their school uniforms, and look out the window to see it's raining again. How do you feel right now? The same way you felt when this last happened?

You have a choice to change this. Every moment you use negative energy in any situation, you affect your mind and body balance, which effects your long-term health.

Stress manifests in your body in different ways. Sometimes, it is fatigue, anger, IBS, or a manifestation of a fear or phobia to limit us from the situation that makes us stressed.

You think I'm exaggerating?

Time Loss

....

16 February 2010

Are you lost in time? What time is it? I'm late! You're late! I'm in a rush. Can't talk or stop just now. I'm going to the gym. Just got to make time?

From the minute you wake up to your alarm, whether human, phone, or bedside clock, to the minute you go to bed, time is our day. And for those of you who do not sleep very well, time is still present during the night when you check the time and wish you were asleep.

When I was very little and we as a family went on holidays (which usually meant a very long car journey), my favourite question was, "what is the time?" I always wanted to know what time it was. I remember one of my first watches. It had a white wrist strap, and Mickey Mouse told me the time with his big white gloved hands. I loved it!

This was sure to stop my issue with time. Not really, though! (Just got my phone to check what time it was as I'm writing this!) We then go to school, and whilst at primary school, there is a schedule. It was at secondary school that time was a huge thing. Do they still have those homework diaries with the lesson planner in the front? We carried around a diary with this planner that was our day planned out for us. It was the same at university, and in my career world, I was led by media schedules, copy deadlines, and event planners. It was all time-related and for another need, but not for my own personal needs.

I stopped wearing a watch a few years ago. The first time I stopped was just during the day because it would irritate my arm when I was working at my desk. There was the clock on my PC screen, and I always put it back on when I went into a meeting. I was still not without time. In the last twelve months, I have not worn a watch. I use my mobile for only phone calls and odd texts, so it is usually in a bag, not near me. I did not consciously say, "I will stop wearing at watch." It just happened.

They say time is relative, but relative to who and what? Time is relative to you, and what I began to understand is that managing time is not managing it. It is allowing and accepting time. Time is of no importance, for when we live in the current moment of now, we lose our focus on time. And we already know what we focus on we attract. For example, people say, "I never have enough time!" Well, that's right. You won't! When you stop thinking about time, it becomes less important. Now for some of you planners (I was/am one!), you can still plan. You still set goals and targets all relative to time; however, right now, time is not conscious. I have now created in my world (where I still have a diary and three planners for different areas of my life), a time-relative world. It is relative to me and my needs. I wake up with my own body alarm (unless I need to be up exceptionally early and then I require assistance). I know when I want to eat lunch and dinner. What time it is no longer controls me. I control my own time. Imagine a world where time is controlled by you?

Finally, for those of you now reading and asking how this works with school runs and a job to get to and this and that, it is still relative to you. When major changes occur in my life, I know I will require a few adjustments in my control of time.

When time controls you, you feel stressed. Stress steals your time. When you are in control, you are happier. The next time you feel rushed or pressed for time, stop for a second and ask why. Within seconds, you will find the answer. That answer is you.

be endless. be eternal. be now. belifehappy.

Walking to the Core

. . . .

17 February 2010

It had been a while since I checked my ticket - my ticket for this journey called life. After a walk on Saturday, I finished and sat on a bench by the sea. The sun was beautiful, and there was a lovely breeze cooling me after my two-hour walk. The walking is achieving so much. I know it is reaching out to people, and that means a lot to me as I chose the Mental Health Foundation to do my charity trek. It is an area many people have a fight with at some point in their lives. The walking is having other benefits, too. I have always been a walker. I had no idea, like on Saturday, how much my mind and body need this. We all benefit as from our strength within. Our core. And that's what this journey is about: Our core. In love. In health. In mind. In purpose.

When we are zooming about, we start to ignore our core, and that's a bit like ignoring someone you love dearly. Do you see that? It's okay to love you. You are as special and important as someone you love dearly. Walking is what I have found to give to my core. The fresh air, the beauty, the walks, the peace within – and yes, I have still experienced those things when I walked along the A15 and around the villages back at home in the UK! Amongst the car fumes! Peace is not the same as quiet. I can still hear the sound of the sea and the noise of building work or traffic when I walk, except for some reason, I stop hearing when I walk since I have my peace.

I'm a big vision and kinaesthetic person, so seeing and feeling things is how I communicate and receive information around me. My hearing switching off when I walk makes sense to me. (Just for my NLP friends: Yes, there was just a bit of auditory digital just there.) Understanding how you communicate is very helpful in our relationships at home, at work, in school, and socially with friends. If you were to say to me, "Did you hear ... I heard ... Have a listen to this ... Did you hear that sound," let's just say I'm going to switch off at some point after you said the word *hear!* However, to say, "I love listening to Jason Mraz," I just felt the word *love.*

So do I hear anything when I'm walking? No! I do see and feel. Ask yourself how you look after your core?

Chaos Theory

· ·

18 February 2010

The chaos theory is as follows: "It has been said that something as small as the flutter of a butterfly's wing can ultimately cause a typhoon halfway around the world." [1]

A butterfly symbolises many things, from the personification of a person's soul to symbolising rebirth. In Ancient Greek, the word *butterfly* was referenced to mean *soul* and *mind*. Butterflies are important as agents in pollination, and in the case here, the belifehappy green butterfly symbolises the spreading of happiness and inspiration.

While researching over the weekend, I was drawn to the chaos theory. Appearing in a search online, I started to feel intrigued and became more interested when I saw it is also known as the "butterfly effect". *The flapping wing represents a small change in the initial condition of the system, which causes a chain of events leading to large-scale phenomena. While the butterfly does not cause the tornado in the sense of providing the energy for the tornado, it does cause it in the sense that the flap of its wings is an essential part of the initial conditions resulting in a tornado, and without that flap, that particular tornado would not have existed.* [2]

---

[1] Butterfly effect, from Wikiquote, 3 December 2014
     http://en.wikiquote.org/wiki/The_Butterfly_Effect
[2] Butterfly effect, from Wikipedia, 14 February 2010,
     http://en.wikipedia.org/wiki/Butterfly_effect

What does this mean to you and me? In the simplest terms, we each have an effect on the world with each action and thought. Each breath. Each word spoken. Each smile. Everything you do has an effect on something else. It's huge, and I think that's pretty hard to get my head around. Although I understand it now, it has taken some practice. It's hard to see you are a part of a bigger picture and then to see that you are whole and the picture is in you. It goes back to the simple statement of "we create our world." What we do or don't do creates our world. Our thoughts when negative breed negativity. So when you think of positive actions and emotions, your butterfly wings become part of a chain of events that lead to more positive actions and emotions. Just by simply smiling at a friend or a stranger, you are offering hope and love to that person as your wing flutters past them. In turn, that person then carries with them during their day the feeling of hope and love and flutters his or her wings with all the people that person interacts with on that same day. One smile.

Imagine knowing today, tomorrow, and every day that you are offering a positive butterfly effect.

Love: Time to Balance and Be You

· ·

22 April 2010

What would happen if you keep breathing in? You inhale, inhale, inhale? With no release, there is no balance of oxygen and carbon dioxide. We unconsciously inhale and exhale to keep a balance in our body.

If you were to sit and listen to your body right now, do you feel any blocks? Perhaps a pain in your body or a tightness in a muscle. Why is it there? Your unconscious mind will not lie to you! So it is up to us to decide if what we are experiencing is an imbalance.

Like breathing, we don't think about each time we breathe. It just happens, and I am sure we are all very thankful for that. Again, though, when we experience periods of anxiety, stress, or depression, we will not first of all say to ourselves "That's it I'm stressed and exhausted I need to allow myself to rest." We instead start to complain of feeling tired and not knowing why. Then we feel nauseous, random pains appear in our joints, and our muscles become tense. That will be because we lifted something heavy last week.

We naturally make excuses for how our body is working or not working. We excuse the imbalance since we know only in ourselves from our unconscious mind that we created the imbalance.

Let's go back to the breathing. Inhale. Exhale. Inhale. Exhale. With one comes the other. A balance. Now look at your daily life and everything from inside, as well as the things outside that are out of your control. Are you in balance?

When we feel anxious or stressed, we are allowing ourselves to feel this way. As we take in more stress or place ourselves in situations where we feel anxious, we inhale and inhale and inhale the stress and anxiety. What are you exhaling? Where is the balance? And what is the balance?

This is where we create blocks internally. The block is our physical warning of an imbalance: where you start to feel tired, don't want to eat your dinner, and really just want to go to bed and not get out for a few days. By listening to our bodies and accepting when something doesn't feel right, we can ask we are feeling this way. You will know by the answer what you require.

Our human body, its systems, and its mechanics reflect our consciousness. Things maybe defined differently; however, they remain the same. We live inside incredible machines that work in conjunction and in balance. So why do we sometimes forget and take for granted the balance of our systems? By being aware and thankful for its work, we give back, thereby creating a balance. By taking a five-minute break of peace and stillness, we give balance.

Exercise: A Short Internal Balancing Exercise

• •

When you are balanced within, your world is in balance.

Now, allow yourself five minutes. Switch off your mobile phone and find somewhere quiet. Let the day drift away, and read this simple relaxation to refresh and balance your mind and body. Likewise, you could ask a friend or a partner to read it to you.

The *Yellow Rose Light* was inspired by a gift I received from my dad later in the year after he died. I'd come down into the kitchen in the morning and walked over to switch on the kettle, as I did and do every morning. Over to the cupboard to get my dotty china tea cup and then back to the kettle. It was then I did a double take. I moved to stand in front of the sink and looked out of the window towards the hedge that bordered the back garden. It was all green except for one yellow rose flower. It was all green yesterday and the day before. Today though it appeared there was a yellow rose, just one, about two feet up, nestled in the hedge. With disbelief at there being only one flower, I went out into the garden in my dressing gown and flip flops. I felt the dewy grass as I walked over, and there, sure enough was one yellow rose.

Now, how it grew over night I have no explanation. Had I just not noticed it before? The reason I know it was a gift was the feeling I felt inside. Love.

Yellow Rose Light (inspired by my dad and his gift of a yellow rose)

Sitting or lying comfortably, with your hands by your side, you close your eyes and start to feel relaxed. All of the day disappearing, floating away, and you see yourself, sitting still, rested. You become aware of your breathing. Become aware of you and your body's balance. Inhale. Now exhale. Take a deep breath in, and slowly exhale. Slow your breathing to a calm balance. Feel calm. Be calm.

Now imagine beautiful yellow light surrounding you. All around you is this beautiful yellow light. Feel its warmth and love. Now inhale this beautiful yellow light. Let its warmth, love, and light travel and flush through your body. Now exhale slowly. Exhale, letting go of all the tension, the worry, and the stress of today. Keep the balance.

Now inhale again the warmth of this light. Inhale the love, and feel it fill your body from your head down to the ends of your toes. Now exhale, letting go, releasing, and relaxing. Enjoy this moment of releasing your worry, your stress, and your anxiety. It is all going and leaving you now. Focus on the balance of your breathing as you inhale and exhale. Breathe slowly. Breathe calmly.

Still with your eyes closed. One, two, three: Wriggle your toes. Four. Open your eyes. Five. Wide awake and feeling refreshed and alive! All your cells are singing warmth, love and happiness.

Allow yourself time to do this every morning or anytime you wish to revitalise your body and maintain your balance of mind and body.

be balance. be health. be peace. be joy. be love. be life. be happy.

Love: I Can't Get No Sleep

29 April 2010

You've tried counting sheep years ago, one, two, three, and even pausing whilst one or two of them missed the stile and went back to jump over it again. Hot chocolate before bed, warming and calming. What else is there? Turning your partner over when they snore. Light on? Light off? Up and down all night.

After a bad night's sleep, the morning is in one way a relief. In another way, you just feel tired. Do you always feel tired? Do you wish you could sleep just one night? Or are you one of the few who sleeps each night? Whatever sleep pattern you have, let's look at some of the reasons for not sleeping and ten tips on improving the quality of your sleep.

With the exclusion of specific illness and medication, many people experience a lack of sleep due to lifestyle in the main. Life has changed: Our environment and requirements in life have changed, and our physical and mental requirements have changed and family life to an extent. It is out of our individual control. When was the last time you thought about your lifestyle and how it was affecting your sleep?

You end each day getting into bed. Snuggle under the duvet and nothing. Eyes open, wide awake. It's infuriating.

So what is stopping you from sleeping?

Touch therapies are relaxing treatments that, with regular (maintained) treatments, will aid improved sleep. It comes back to balance, of which touch therapies work on rebalancing the mind and body. A rested mind means a rested body. Therefore, a stressed mind equals a stressed body.

Does it mean you are stressed if you do not sleep? Not necessarily. I'm using the term *stressed* here as some of my clients and people I speak to use that word (unfortunately!) Anything that troubles the mind will trouble our body. So to get sleep, the body and mind require a balanced state. A calm neutral state allows both mind and body to rest. (I'm guessing like your laptop in hibernate mode.)

Ten tips to help get the sleep you want

Clear the clutter in your bedroom

Check under your bed, on the bedside table, and in your wardrobe. Make your bedroom a sanctuary for you.

Open the windows

When you can, leave the windows in your bedroom open for a few hours. Let your room breathe.

Check your mattress

You spend on average of six to eight hours of your day in bed asleep (when you sleep!) You are worth a mattress that is right for you. Turn it, and air it. Consider investing in a new one.

Music

Play relaxing music. Get into bed, lie on your back, and focus on the music. Listen to the music as you relax and float off to sleep.

Thank your day

When you get into bed, settle in, lie on your back, think of everything in your day, and say thank you. Say thank you for your health, happiness, family, friends, and the people at work. This will help you let go of today, clearing your mind.

Balance

For those of you stationary most of your day at a desk, make time at lunch or after work to go for a stroll around the block or do some kind of exercise. For those of you active during your day, take five to sit and relax with no music, TV, or anything. Just you.

Talk and write it out

When something is troubling, your mind talks. Talk to a friend, family member, or partner, or write the problem out. The key is to stop the pattern. Think about finding a solution. Don't pressure yourself. You might need to make steps towards a solution. The first step will help ease and rest your mind.

Laugh

Isn't it just the best medicine? Have a laughter night where you get comedy movies. Laugh with your children. Find your inner child just for a moment and let all your worries go and laugh and play. Stand wherever you are, and say to yourself, "I am happy." Repeat ten times, and feel the smile come across your face. (Others will see it, too!)

Variety

Bring variety into your day. Allowing your mind and body to experience new sounds, sights, and tastes distracts, grows, and rests your mind. It is all about choice. Allow yourself to experience new things and give yourself more choice.

Relax

You are special. The feeling of touch is soothing, nurturing, and relaxing. It calms the nervous system and the mind. Have pamper-me time, and allow yourself this special time once a week. Remember many complementary touch therapies all promote relaxation and improve sleep over a period of time and with regular treatments.

We are given choice, and we have the choice to stay the same. To create change can be sudden or gradual. Changing lifestyle habits is a change for life. A lifetime of happiness. Sleep well.

Give: What Is Giving?

....

4 May 2010

Giving: What does it really mean? Is it about money, or is it about time or love or other things? To give, by definition, can sometimes be a bit vague. What about giving to yourself? How can we do that?

It is strange, really, because when you immediately hear the word *give*, you associate it with an external action. I wonder how many of you reading this will be thinking of giving to yourself? And can giving to someone else or an organisation be giving to you, as well? Most of our giving actions will unconsciously balance with receiving simply because we work in balance. When you feel unhappy or have a grievance towards giving, then the question is whether you are giving in the right way for you? There are many ways you can give:

Money
Time
Assistance
Your skills
Volunteering
Fundraising

Then, there are:

Kindness
Love
Comfort
Rest

Relaxation

Listening

People who fundraise for charities will be drawn to organisations that research, support, and promote a cause that they have been affected by, directly or indirectly. It is a way of giving in memory or support and with thanks.

I was drawn to help support the Mental Health Foundation for these reasons. There is still some way to go in terms of stigma; however, people are becoming more aware of mental illness, action, and available treatments. I realised that one of my greatest mental escapes was walking and decided to do my first charity trek this year to give to a charity so I could give thanks.

Play: Find Your Inner Child

5 May 2010

Think about the laughter of a child. The infectious pure laughter and smile, of innocence, of now. Enjoying the fullness of the moment. The playful, joyful sound of laughter.

Amongst our daily responsibilities, we can forget our innocence, our inner child. As days pass and weeks pass, we forget. So what can we do to play and bring our inner child into daily living.

What brings you joy? Write a list of people, activities, books, music, movies, and places that bring you joy. From this list, you might even find that your daily work is one of your joys.

When was the last time you did any of the items on your list? With the list in front of you, you can now plan how you can bring these things into your life every day, thereby bringing joy into your day.

I spent a recent afternoon with my nephew. We danced and sung our hearts out to a film we were watching. We laughed so much as we became rock stars. In that moment, there was nothing but happiness. To be and allow yourself to have that joy is a gift, something many of us do not allow ourselves because we are busy and there are other things to do.

What would happen if you laughed more? (I'd love right now to hear all your answers.) I'm sitting here, smiling. Laughter is music.

Play. We had playtime at school. We played with our friends. We played games. We played in teams. We played music. As we grow, do we stop playing? Playtime changes from creative imaginations to creative holiday planning or creative home/gardening DIY. How else do we play?

We have a world full of creatively inspired playtime, and we can find joy in everything we do. Look at your world, and ask how you can play today.

be playful. be joy. be laughter. be love. be life. be happy. belifehappy.

List: What Brings Me Joy

(This page is all yours!)

Love: Finding and Growing

. . . .

6 May 2010

Today is about love. Love for yourself. Finding and growing it.

Love is everywhere in our world, and love for ourselves is often something we don't prioritise. We have love for others, and we neglect ourselves. Without love for ourselves, we surely have less to give.

Belief is fuelled by love. Everything comes back to love. Have you asked where this source of love is? When you have asked, you will know the source is you. Love is a journey to the top of the mountain; as we approach it, we believe in ourselves to reach the top, and as we climb it, we are protected and motivated to reach the peak we know we are: love. The work in reaching the top is not easy, and finding ways to care for ourselves requires us to allow ourselves to love: you.

And this is the hardest thing. The ultimate achievement to love is in what we see and feel today, tomorrow, and every day. Each day requires work. Over time, the changes, the results, and the gifts appear. We see out over the mountain, absorbing the beauty of the view.

Finding ways to bring love into our daily lives is a learning process. Believing in love will make a difference and is perhaps the first step. Then there is the wonder of what and where it will take us.

There are many ways we can allow love into our lives, from simple meditative, quiet time to tai chi or other activities and complementary therapies. Anything that gives you joy is giving you time to love yourself.

Love is all encompassing, a pulsing flow of rose petal pink light flowing through your body from head to toe. It is pulsing waves of pink light, slowly filling all of your body, energising, caring, and healing your body. Sit still, and allow this light to surround you. It wraps around you, and you feel as though your worries are drifting away. This is love. Love all encompassing. Love unconditional. You are love. I am love. We are love. Breathe in this beautiful, loving pink light now. Be love.

Believe you are protected, safe, and loved today, tomorrow, and every day.

be you. be love. be life. be happy. belifehappy.

Are You Comfortable in Your Zone?

. . . .

10 May 2010

I know (and I'm included) that many of you reading this have a comfort zone. The comfort might be a thing that provides comfort in a place, a person, a job, etc. Jumping outside the comfort zone is a testing time and only to us individually. I've spent the last two weeks out of my comfort zone and proved to myself so many things on different levels across different areas of my life.

Not unusual is the comfort of our own bed, and for me, it is also my sofa (although I don't spend that much time on it – when I do, I grab half an hour, and it is my heaven of comfort!). Other areas of comfort we find are in our general environment, the people we are with, and the conversations we have. After spending the last six months readjusting my life, this recent trip back to the UK has showed me what life was like before and how I would manage it. I did. You really do not get the opportunity to avoid and bury things in your life! They will come back in some form for you to either accept or continue to fight off. I have no more fight! And I found myself further along the path of forgiveness and acceptance. Have you heard these words before? "It's OK. I'm OK with it. It's sorted." Was it? Was it really? Having used the words for years and then during this trip hearing others saying it, I realised there were some things in my own life that still required complete acceptance. How easy it is really to just let go?

Flip this round now! We all can look at a situation that we have buried, and look at our daily lives in words spoken, music, and how we feel physically, and ask what you have to learn from this? When you don't hear the answer, keep going! Giving up will just let the situation come back! The answer is always inside: How much do you want to find the answer?

After acceptance in my personal relationships zone, I was comfortable again! That doesn't mean there are no more zones, though. We all have challenges to our comfort. Are you looking to keep your life inside your zone, or are you seeking ways to expand your zone?

Our internal confidence has a lot to do with how far we will push our own personal zones. Later this year, I am flying to China. I have flown quite often and find being up in the sky a relaxing time. This, however, will be my longest flight, and this takes me out of my home zone. Where once I would dedicate sometime to worry about this, I now understand this will not change the outcome. I am flying to China. Fact. Worry apportioned to this event is simply wasted, so I accept the fact!

Social comfort zones including networking are all together another thing. Many of us find our confidence is tested in terms of meeting new people, speaking in public groups, and even in situations with people we have known for years. Overcoming this comfort zone has the same process as others. Get your spade, and let's start digging! What is it that allows you to feel out of your comfort zone? Why? And what would you do if you did not feel out of your comfort zone?

Step outside of you when you ask these questions. Let your true self speak.

Our comfort zones are a baseline in basic need of security and safety, and that's a positive! Maintaining the zones can require work on our part to protect us from experiencing new things, learning, and growing. This is a choice on our part. We also have the choice to learn and grow and expand our comfort zones.

Do you listen to the same radio station every morning on the way to work? This is an example of a comfort zone. What would happen if you tuned into a different one on the way home from work tonight? This really is the simplest of changes to a comfort zone in your life. We have a choice on how we manage and expand our individual zones.

A comfort zone is a limitation of your world. Work with your comfort zones, and feel your world expand with new views, new experiences, and new choices.

It is your world. be you. be life. be happy.

Give: Understanding How You Can Help

. . . .

11 May 2010

The challenge ahead of me is approaching, and the reality of the trek is getting closer into my vision. Whilst I have been training since the New Year, I feel the next four months will fly by.

Training takes another new level now as I start using walking poles and increased weight in my rucksack. Determination is the best word I can give you to describe how I feel about this personal walking challenge. And the challenge is not just the physical training to ensure that I am able to complete the task. The challenge has now become so much more: about sharing with you and many others I meet about mental health and how we look after our mind/body balance.

Knowing I am able to reach more people to share the light at the end of the tunnel is my gift to give.

Ten years ago, the attitude in society, in the workplace, and in the world in general was to not discuss stress or depression, let alone use the words *mental illness*. Dementia was perhaps more acceptable as this was a perception of elderly people, so that was okay. Ten years on, and I hear from people with depression or from people supporting others with depression, and it is so wonderful to hear them say that they are not afraid to tell people what they are experiencing and of all the support they are receiving from relatives, friends, and professional medical support.

One lady described her experience as the closest she has been to hell in all her life and that she believed this happened only to other people. This is such a common belief. I believe, as one of the others it happened to in a time of high stigma, I was given the opportunity to turn my world from the darkest depths of being forced underground in a world with no light, to a world years later, standing on top of the highest mountain breathing in the brightest light.

We all have the ability to give a gift of our time, our support, our kindness, and our love.

More and more people are turning on their light to help and give to others, and this is why we are able to openly speak of helping our heroes, some of whom experience posttraumatic stress disorder. Just by understanding we help. Learning and sharing creates awareness, and awareness grows.

We all choose our own way in which we can give to help others. Simply inviting a friend for a cup of tea and a chat can make a difference. If you don't know how to help friends or family members, ask. They will tell you. They might even ask for you to leave them to have some time or ask you to go to the supermarket with them. Some of the things they ask you to do you might feel are insignificant, but to your friends, it will be all the difference from the darkness to knowing and believing they have people who care and are there to help them with the little things.

Give your gift of a smile, and shine your brightness to everyone around you.

Thank you.

be thankful. be kind. be support. be patient. be love. be life. be happy.

Play: Dancing Through The Fields

....

12 May 2010

Inspired in play today by two dancing butterflies. They danced for what seemed like hours across the top of the long grass, with a bright blue sky as their backdrop. Happy, light and fluttering in front of my eyes, I had to press pause on my walk to notice the playfulness.

Get active and bring play into your day

Dancing is not just for the professionals! Dancing is something you can do on your own at home, with your friends, children or partner. You can join a dance group to learn and meet new people. Dancing doesn't feel natural for everyone, however with so many instruments and artists - we all love music as a vibration of life.

Get creative inspiring your mind

Writing stories, journals, and your thoughts stimulates your mind and creates an outlet of expression, releasing emotions and ideas and opening your mind - boosting your creativity.

Get away and play

Change is as good as a rest. A break can rest your mind from daily routines and inspire with new air, new places, and new faces. Your break can be whatever you want it to be. A walk around your local woods or park, a weekend break, or a two-week vacation. Allowing yourself to experience a new environment or a break from your daily routine can be just the break you need.

Create your own smiles and play in your day.

be creative. be inspired. be play. be joy. be life. be happy.

Love: You

· ·

13 May 2010

In our lifetime, we proclaim to love another and others. How many of us proclaim to love ourselves? And for those astounded by the question, please stay with me here. Discover just how simply you can begin to give love to yourself and feel and see the full experience and benefits loving yourself ignites across your life and throughout your world.

When you feel love, what are those feelings? What do you feel? Where do you feel the feelings of love? What do you see, and how do you see love? What do you hear, and what sounds does love make? What do you taste, and how does love smell? Light up your senses towards love, and awaken your love of *you*.

Loving ourselves is not a headline or often found on a priority list. Why? Love can be referred to as something we give externally to others. It is an exchange of giving and then receiving. Or do we? Many people who experience disease, anxiety, depression, and low self-esteem have at some point neglected themselves of love. It is a very easy thing to do (to stop loving who we are), and it is a very easy thing to start loving you again today, tomorrow, every day.

Bringing love into your day and to you is simply awareness and balance. Control, gratitude, thanks, giving, and receiving.

By taking control, we take back the power to drive our focus into what we actually desire in our day-to-day lives. From a simple decision of I am leaving work an hour earlier than usual to I will apply for the promotion/job today.

Decisions irrelevant of the impact of change, all can create change. Take back the control by taking decisions today, tomorrow, every day. You will find the result of your decision-making gives you more time in your day to love you.

Gratitude for our life and everything in our life is an awareness of ourselves. By reminding ourselves each day what we are thankful for, we acknowledge, learn, accept, and are grateful for. We then move on.

Again, it is another way for us to allow more time into our life. Start with a list of the things you are thankful about yourself:

I am thankful for my health.
I am thankful for my legs so I can walk for charity.
I am thankful for my fingers so I can write.

Your own personal gratitude list will become endless as you become more aware of who you are. Start a list to be thankful for people in your life and other areas of your life. Once you start this list, you will be surprised at what you are thankful for. You can write one of these lists at any time or even to help you relax in the evening, on the way home from work, in the bath or shower, or when you get into bed. Simply say thank you for the events and people you have encountered that day.

So far, you have a list of how you feel; what you see, hear, taste, and smell when you think about love; a list of actionable statements or decisions of simple actions you can start taking; and a list of what and who you are thankful for. What have you achieved in that short time?

Awareness

Awareness of you. You have given yourself time to be aware of who you are. That is love. A simple step to loving you today, tomorrow, and every day.

be love. be life. be happy.

Turnaround

17 May 2010

Welcome to another amazing week, day, and moment. Do you feel the amazingness right now? Stop and breathe it all in. Just how big is that amazingness right now?

Turn around your day. Last week, in the space of twenty-four hours, events in my life were, let's say, not going the way I expected. The way I wanted. Least of all when I dyed my white clothes an off-brown shade! It was not the best experience. Then I was informed I definitely have no TV connection in my apartment, analogue or digital. Not a major thing: My TV functions well as a feature in the lounge! Then in order to rescue my clothes, I had to bike to the next village. Okay, I began to feel a little fed up. Knowing there was nothing I could do except get my bike out, I headed off up the hill. Ouch. I was test driving a car that morning. A car I had happened to walk by the day before and was the make and model I had been looking for. I walked in (parked my bike!).

As I waited for a lady to come down to the garage to come with me on the test drive, I sat and talked to the owner. We talked about what I do and enjoy doing. He asked, "Do you play golf?"

What I'm trying to explain is that from the disaster of my clothes washing to the uphill battle on my bike, this question presented an opportunity for me, and I saw it. Had I been stressed and upset that my clothes were presently a lovely new shade of off-brown at home in my washing machine, and my personal fitness being a constant battle for me as I aim to be the best I have ever been (breathe), I would have missed this opportunity. How many opportunities do we miss simply because we woke up in the morning and spilt milk on our shirt? By simply letting go of that moment, we can enjoy every moment fully.

The thing I am learning is when I am not really thinking about anything, my life goes really smoothly. Opportunities fly through my door. It then becomes a question of how to manage this every day.

You can turn around any moment, event, or comment. What just happened? My clothes are an off-brown (some were new, if this can add to my moment of despair). What can you do to correct it? Bike to the shop, and buy a corrective washing powder. How do you feel now? Okay. Being aware of the questions and process of learn, accept, resolve, leave, and move on, I was able to do just that. Pretty much any part of my day that throws me a good one, I stop for a minute, think of the event, process it, and move on.

In the last six days, I have been sent many experiences, people, and events to test my process. Going on how I would have reacted before, this new way is much less time-consuming, so I get to enjoy my day today, tomorrow, and every day.

Before you react, think about what has just happened. Turn around events and see the opportunities fly through your door.

be positive. be proactive. be acceptance. be gratitude. be life. be happy.

P.S. My clothes are white again! And from the conversation with the car sales man, I was connected with the owner of a local golfing range who kindly allowed me to host a fundraising event for the Mental Health Foundation.

Give: A Helping Hand

. . . .

18 May 2010

Finding some days when we feel nothing is going our way, from the morning through to the end of the day, feels like rubbish. The next day is the same. Whilst we share a little laugh now and again, in a month's time, we wonder when the last time we laughed was. You see your friends less often, opting for sleeping or simply doing nothing. As the weeks pass, you start to realise you don't even want to answer your text messages, let alone a phone call. For now and this minute, just going to work and doing the basic errands is enough. Dinner is ready, and today, you watch yourself push your food around your plate, maybe one mouthful, because you simply can't be bothered to eat. Everything takes time. Do I really need to wash my hair? More time. One day and the next is a daze. A numb daze.

Then there it is right in front of you. Yes, you in the mirror. That is you in the mirror, except you don't see you. You see someone else. Suddenly, you are no longer you. You are trapped inside a mind and body that is no longer communicating. Scared. Who on earth will understand? Have I gone mad? Am I having one of those breakdowns people talk about? Goodness, I feel like I haven't eaten in months. How did I not eat? I can't speak. Even this is too much to do.

The day when help is realised is the day the tears fall, and the numbness alters to allow an emptiness of you. You know you are empty, and you know you want help.

The above is my account and experience of depression. Everyone will have their own individual experience, and that is one in four of us who will be affected by mental illness at some point in our life. Once, we heard of someone with depression months or years ago, and now, it is common to hear of someone you know who is currently experiencing stress, anxiety, or being treated for depression. For those who have been the other three and have not experienced this, it is similar to being trapped in a hole that I can only liken to the early 1980's children's programme *Jamie and the Magic Torch* with his slide (except here there is no torch), spiralling down, and it can take months and months to realise you are ill. Believing the aches and pains are from something else, the frequent colds are hay fever or maybe the air conditioning system at work. Everything is just an off day until it just becomes a blur.

Spotting the signs are difficult as we are all individuals. Signs of stress and anxiety are most common now, and people are more likely to talk about it. Getting help and asking for help; we all still have a long way to go.

Offering a helping hand is a way for you to give. As you give your help, your friend, family member, or colleague will acknowledge and receive your kindness. This starts a process. Once people receive, after feeling totally isolated, they know there is help. As they ask more, you give them more strength. With more strength, their confidence grows. As you give more confidence, they start to return to everyday errands. As you give them living, they will give you love and joy.

You can choose to give support and your kindness daily. In return, you will receive joy daily. Think about your friends and your family. Is there someone who has asked for your help but maybe you didn't have time? Allow yourself time to make a drink and pick up the telephone. Call them. Write them an email. Get out and visit them. Giving yourself time to help others gives help to you.

There will be times when you offer help, and it is refused; this is not because your help is not good enough. It is simply that the friend is not ready for help yet. Always be available to help others when they are ready for it. We all find people, the right people, to help us when we are ready. Be patient, and they appear, sometimes miraculously. They are just the right person, at the right time, saying the right thing, and giving the right help.

Your hand waves hello and goodbye, it wipes away tears, it soothes pain, it protects you and your loved ones, it makes things, and it moves things. Your hands are amazing. Give a helping hand today.

belifehappy.

Play: Holiday Vision Board Party with Survival Tips

....

19 May 2010

The smell of warm air, the gentle touch of the warm air breeze tickling your skin – splash! Laughter. Where are you?

We work hard, and there is always time to play! However, why did holidays get so stressful? Is there a way to enjoy the whole process of booking, preparing, and being away on any kind of escape?

First of all, a definition of a holiday (because we really do have different views of what a holiday is):

noun 1: an extended period of recreation, especially away from home. 2: a day of festivity or recreation when no work is done.[3]

(Recreation is an enjoyable leisure activity.)

A great way to get your friends and family involved in planning a holiday is creating your very own holiday vision board. Why not? We talk about them for our lives; why not for a holiday? The fun starts here. Invite everyone who is going on the trip to your home, and ask everyone to bring magazines, newspapers, and holiday brochures. Find a large cardboard box or ask at your local supermarket (about

---

[3]   *Oxford English Dictionary*, s.v. "holiday"

A2), some A4 card, too, sticky glue, blu-tack, sellotape and scissors. Pop on some happy holiday music, and get creating!

Focused

Is there a budget? Agree on your budget first to make the creativity realistic. Then get started by asking everyone to make a small board for themselves. What is their holiday choice? Places, activities, food, drink, entertainment, and climate. After half an hour, everyone should have their personal holiday.

Fun

See from each person's board what similarities you have on destinations, climate, and activities, and start to create your group holiday vision board. Let's go!

Faith

By creating your holiday together in this way, everyone will enjoy it. You all created it!

I thought it would also be helpful to share with you some tips on how to create your holiday (playtime) without the stress to help you have a belifehappy holiday.

Your destination

You always have a choice on the type of holiday, who it is with, and how much: Get your vision board!

Packing

Roll your clothes in your baggage for less creasing (much easier to unpack, too!).

Journey

Plan your journey in advance. Allow yourself time and build some stops in if required.

Entertainment

Plan entertainment for you and everyone else traveling. Ask what everyone wants to do.

By air?

If traveling by air, take your time at the airport. Accept that there will be a queue at the check-in desk. Enjoy the queue!

Managing delays

Are you delayed or stuck in a jam? Play the "How many happy words do I know" game? Sounds a bit happy? It will have you all happy!

People

It's your break, and yet, there are other passengers on your journey. That's okay. Be respectful of their space, and if they are not of yours, it is an experience they are creating. You enjoy your experience.

You've arrived

On arrival at your destination, smile. You have arrived on your break!

Enjoy!

Each day, ask yourself and the people traveling with you what you would all like to do in your day. You are not responsible for other people's happiness. You are able to give people a choice, and you also have a choice. Listen, decide, and then enjoy!

Returning home with a smile

Repeat these steps on the return!

Wishing you belifehappy holidays.

Love: Focused Energy, Focused Needs

20 May 2010

Focusing our energy towards what we are passionate about is love. Where is your energy focused, and how does it make you feel? Our lives can be packaged into key areas of health and fitness, social, relationships, career, financial and well-being. And whilst we have these compartments, how often do we review how we actually feel about them? And how would we know when we looked? We might just find the answer we were looking for.

The only limits we have are the limits we place on ourselves. Is that love? We have basic (physiological) needs as Abraham Maslow pointed in his Hierarchy of Needs (from the bottom to top):

Physiological

Breathing, food, water, reproduction, sleep, homeostasis (balance), excretion

Safety

Security of body (self), employment, resources, morality, the family, health, property

Love and Belonging

Friendship, family, sexual intimacy

Esteem

Self-esteem, confidence, achievement, respect for others, respect by others

Self-actualization

Morality, creativity, spontaneity, problem solving, lack of prejudice, acceptance of facts

Our basic needs are required to be in balance in order for us to have security, and with security in our life, we can have love. With love, we have confidence, and with confidence, we can solve problems and be creative, nonjudgmental, and accepting.

Another way to look at this is our everyday lives. Where is your energy focused, and how do you feel? When we are focused on something that we are not in alignment with, some of our basic physiological needs may be neglected a little (for instance, not drinking enough fluid and missing meals). The security in some areas of your life may also feel less as this focus draws your energy away from these needs. Love through friendships, family, and relationships may also be affected. You start to lose respect for others and yourself, and self actualisation seems a million miles away. So let's go back to the bottom to your physiological needs.

We are so complex and yet so simple to rebalance through our basic needs. Tiredness (insomnia, aches and pains, and joint stiffness) to stomach discomfort will more often than not be traced back to one or more of your basic needs. Call it homeostasis, balance, inner balance, holistic balance, or basic needs – it is one of the same.

We do not have to wait for someone to love us before we are able to love ourselves as it might appear in stage three of Maslow's hierarchy. In fact, being in love with yourself (especially our single friends) draws love to you. Look at it another way. When you are able to maintain balance in yourself, you feel, look and sound amazing. You will bounce through hallways, train stations, buses, and out with your friends. When you focus your energy on what you really are passionate about, you are in alignment. In balance. You are in love with yourself, because you are love. How awesome!

With so many areas and needs to fulfil in our life, there are times when focusing on one area can leave you feeling a little depleted in another. The fear creeps up inside you, and you remain with a small internal battle on your hands. Refocus now. That's right: Get your lens, and start to turn. As we change our thoughts and our focus, we sometimes leave parts of us behind. By actually refocusing, you will catch up and be one. In balance.

There are many holistic treatments that support you through these refocussing/rebalancing times, such as reiki, holistic massage, reflexology, acupressure, shiatsu, and other treatments, and therapy including yoga that work within our energy meridians. You can also find that a simple walk will help your mind and body balance. All of these things help us release the energy we no longer wish to hold onto. The energy that is pulling us back. Breathe out, and let go of the energy left behind that is still within, and breathe in your focused energy. Where you are and want to be and do and have. Allow through love time to rebalance, and give love to yourself to continue to give your love to others.

be focused. be balance. be releasing. be love. belifehappy.

In the Flow

· ·

24 May 2010

I've spent a few days in the last week walking and was lucky enough to be invited to a small village in the hills on Saturday. After a wonderful drive there, (the views as we went higher where simply amazing and a Cyprus not many get to appreciate), we arrived at our destination, a cafe. As I sat down, I instantly felt relaxed. This was life. Simple. We had a drink, and it turned colder, and we moved inside whilst our food was being cooked. Accompanied by a flat screen on the wall with local TV, the rest of the room was simple. The television programmes were a luxury to me. What I realised in that moment was the peace, tranquillity, and simplicity was around me and within me. The birds flew above our heads into their nest and out again, and five hours later, after superb food, we drove back down to the coast before sunset.

As I walked back from the shops collecting my weekend newspapers, I looked around each corner, still learning my way around this old part of the village where I now live. (I just typed *love* before I typed *live*!). I remembered the peach-coloured house, and as I turned, I looked again, seeing two rows of beautiful sunflowers upright. They even looked like they were greeting me and smiling. I smiled and walked along the next road, and all I could see was the beautiful green trees lining the road and the stunningly bright flowers waving me through and down the road ahead. For that moment, I was the road, the trees, the flowers, and the breeze. It was all flowing through me.

I looked around again and thought back to the day in the hills. For these moments, I was in the flow. The flow of life. My life. And now having fully experienced that flow and the moment in complete consciousness, I feel more alive than ever before.

I am what is around me. I am the warm breeze, the peace, the calmness, the beauty, and brightness of nature. I am simplicity and tranquillity. I am my own road to happiness today, tomorrow, and every day.

I've found myself with this new experience reviewing the last five months. We sometimes forget or miss our achievements and the goals we set out at the beginning of the year, and I realised with some peace around me that I could do just that. I'm ticking off things, that's for sure, as I moved house, I officially completed my reiki master certification, and I have settled into my new life. So far, so good! The next six months hold for me to walk on the Great Wall of China for the Mental Health Foundation and for me to step into my light and stand in my love.

The review has been worth the personal time investment. I have learnt a lot that I have been able to release and let go and to finally realise through my own fear that I have been holding back a huge personal opportunity. I am now feeling so much better, both physically and mentally, as I am one again with my focus completely aligned with me. Like holding three pieces of ribbon together at the top and smoothing them down together to the bottom. In alignment, becoming one piece of ribbon.

To be in the flow, in alignment, and in balance helps each of us review, appreciate, be grateful, and move onwards brighter and happier. The stream runs into the river, and the river joins the sea. All flowing.

Loving the flow and the learning, and wishing you all a very awesomely fabulously flowing day.

Give: Without Reason

. . . .

25 May 2010

What will you do today that will change a moment in someone else's day? Will you offer your seat to someone travelling on the tube or the bus? Will you offer to help someone with shopping bags? Will you help a stranger who has fallen in the street? (We will get back to this one!)

Will you make your colleague a cup of tea this morning? Or help them with a project? Will you listen to a friend who has a problem today? Will you spend time playing with your child? Will you visit a family member just for a chat?

There are many, many actions you can chose from today to give to a stranger or colleague, friend, or family member. Giving is help without expecting anything in return. Your help becomes an act of kindness, which with the universal laws, will be returned to you. This is not to say the kindness is to be expected back from the person you helped. It is just that your act of kindness will be repaid when you need it, maybe from someone you have not even met yet.

How would you respond when you see a stranger in distress in a public place? Do you walk on by? Call for help? Go over and offer your help? According to a book I am reading at the moment (*59 Seconds: Think a Little, Change a Lot* by Professor Richard Wiseman), acts of kindness are few in these situations. Why? When there are a large number of people whose attention at this point is drawn to the incident, in most circumstances, people will watch and wait to see what other observers are doing. No action, and no responsibility. When there are only one or two observers, you are more likely to be helped. So where does this leave you when you need help, and there are lots of observers? It is recommended that you look for a friendly face, one you can connect with and explain to (if you can) what help you need. That person will then act (in a sense, you passed the responsibility needed in order to for an individual to act). Look for the friendly face.

So giving isn't a reciprocal action between the same giver and receiver, and when we get caught in the trap of this is what we think, we can become disappointed that a friend or colleague or family member didn't help when we helped them. Giving is without response.

You receive in your life because you give. Giving in this way opens more opportunities for happiness and balance. After helping someone, we feel good unless you are helping only because you feel you have to.

How do you feel about your giving? Do you feel you give too much? Are not receiving? Some of us are so happy giving that we often forget to ask for help, or we refuse help that would in return allows us to accept and receive. By blocking your receiving, we often become upset that we never receive help. In these situations, ask yourself whether you asked for help and if you asked the people who can help you.

Our expectations are often misled when we do not understand how to give. Give openly and allow yourself to receive, remembering that there are people we might not even know yet who will come into our lives to help us when we need it. You know that they were just the right person. Feel and show gratitude for all you receive to complete your balance.

Be the friendly face in the crowd, and step in to help a stranger. Be allowing of yourself to receive others' giving and be grateful for what you receive. You will find more daily happiness from giving with no expectation. The next time you help someone, think for one second afterwards about how you feel.

Every little gesture of your kindness helps another.

be kind. be acceptance. be grateful. be love. be life. be happy.

Love: Your Stage

•••

27 May 2010

Speaking of love is more than just a word. Love has a power that some connect to as a high vibration of energy. As everything moves and everything changes, there are different levels of energy. The lower the vibration, the denser the object is. Love is a pure form of energy that equates in numerology to the number nine (eight plus one equals nine where the *belifehappy* dream started), which is also a high vibrational number, and for some, it is referred to as a spiritual enlightenment.

So love of yourself really does come from within. You are your own source of love. Each of us has a choice to speak to ourselves and to work with our love. Share our love, and receive others' love.

Love is the abundant light. It is the stage spot light within which you stand. The light moves with you as you move around the stage; acting your life; choosing the role you wish to play each day, each hour, each minute. Choosing the script you wish to read from. The light never leaves you; it is constantly moving with you.

Your light fades and brightens according to your control. You have the power of love to control the light. Your mind and body work with love. Love fuels the mind and body, and out of balance, the light will become dim. When you are in harmony, the light shines brightly, emanating your inner light. Your love. That's when other people comment and say, "You look really great today, have you done something different?" You know you have dressed much the same; you just added more light (and love!).

We say we are looking dull when we are ill or unhappy, and this is in reference to your light. The secret is to learn how to maintain your energy and your brightness on stage. We all have a dimmer switch we can flick; however, it is about how you manage to get the brightness back.

To live life as in dark, light, dark, light, dark, light creates unrest in our mind and body and becomes tiring (an everlasting disco). To live in darkness is to have no love. To live with brightness, accepting a few dimmer days is living with love and accepting your control over your light. Finding a stage light you can work with and feel comfortable with is the key. It's your show!

Whilst on stage, acting your life, you have all the props and different stage set screens covering the places, activities, and people you love. You choose these props and sets. Your director allows you to choose. Would you choose something you don't enjoy to join you on your stage? No? Let your stage light guide you now to what props and stage sets you have right now. How do you feel when you look at them? For the props and sets you no longer feel fit in to this act and scene, thank them and work with your director to let them go. As the play continues, new props and new sets will emerge for you to choose.

You've created your stage for today. Your props, your sets, your script, and the brightness of your stage light. You are the director. You call the shots. Be the star of your show today, tomorrow, and every day.

Control your light, and let it guide you effortlessly with your love around your stage.

be love. be life. be happy.

Learning Through The Shift

· ·

31 May 2010

To say this is a time of change is understating. Change is constant; sometimes we notice it and feel it, other times we don't. Right now I'm feeling it!.

What I've found myself doing over the last few days is asking new questions, and a new perspective is developing. A new window in which to look out of. To go back to what is around us, what we have created is interesting for me right now, relating to Buddha's principle of what we think, we become.

So this is what I have been thinking. What thoughts have I been thinking, and how have I created what is around me? What do I want to change to progress my goals? Other situations through conversations or newspaper and magazine articles have led me to discussions about fear in present situations and personal desires for the future. We all have situations of fear; it is the action we take that is important.

It is interesting to read and discuss how people feel towards happiness and what stops people from allowing themselves to live it. It is also interesting because it is a reflection of me and the world I am creating. I'm still learning on that level!

The conversations I feel deeply involved in as I listen to how people are feeling trapped into their lives and understanding their reasons, and it is only a lack of action that holds them back. It is similar to walking yourself into a remote prison cell, locking the door, and throwing the key outside. Why would you do that? Do you really think someone is going to save you?

When the excuses start, others follow until we have convinced ourselves it wasn't for us or our time. Later, we look back and ask ourselves why we didn't do those things. The only person stopping you is you. You just threw the keys to your prison cell out the window! What are you going to do now?

In creating our reality and our desires, included in the thoughts is a safety net. It is invisible to us. The challenge is to jump and trust, because when you fully believe in yourself, you will take a leap and let go of the 'how' and start to allow everything you have been focusing on to happen. The purpose of life is not to get stitched up by someone or something. Only you can do that.

So when I go back to the articles on happiness, I go back to thinking of the days when I created belifehappy back in early 2008. A dream it was, and why belifehappy? These articles are now talking about happiness being likened to a shopping trip: short-term fixes, and that joy is longer lasting as joy is love. Being happy and extending our lifetime as long as we do a list of things, which is the writer's perception of information received. I was surrounded at the time in an environment where all I could see being offered were short term fixes for happiness and all I wanted to know was how could I be happy each day for my lifetime? I'd wasted enough, as far as I was concerned, and now I was ready to start living! I just wanted to live happy and be life happy. Not long after, I found love: the love within. There are so many on a journey, including some of you guys, searching for something. Happiness in my eyes comes only from being honest with yourself. It really doesn't matter what other people want for you or think they want for you. You know inside what will allow you to be happy, whether it is a new career, a new hobby, a new relationship, a new location, and you have control. (What I didn't tell you was when you locked yourself in the remote prison cell, there is a spare key inside your cell. You'll see it when you are ready to see it!)

The world is your world today, tomorrow, and every day. This is your lifetime of happiness, through your choices, acceptance, and love. You create how you balance your mind and body, how you fuel your machine, and what thoughts you have. No one else is responsible, and if you let others make the choices for you, then that was your choice.

A lifetime of happiness involves giving, playing, loving, and learning. belifehappy.

What choices will you make today to create a day filled with happiness?

Give: Effortlessly

. . . .

1 June 2010

Without effort, everything appears to be much easier. So why do we often feel things are such an effort? Did we make them an effort? I read an article this week about giving in terms of continuing to give as one of the ways to happiness. This is similar to when we spoke about giving unconditionally.

This is my first trek and first solo fundraising effort, and I am learning so much. At first, I thought of the training as just getting fitter and giving me an edge to ensure I had the endurance for five solid days of walking. Now each time I walk, I think about the time I am giving to me and others, and with each conversation, I am giving myself the opportunity to speak the truth about people's fears of these two words together (mental health) and for people to have the opportunity to support this great charity.

I have the opportunity to give my time of anywhere around ten hours of walking a week. I give my time to write about my experiences of depression and about how life, in balance of mind and body, has all the possibilities of creating a lifetime of happiness through little changes every day. This includes a smile, a laugh, helping your neighbour, listening to what words you use and replacing them with words of encouragement and positivity, including play and relaxation time in your day, and learning to tune into your love.

I chose to live like this. Simple. I accepted the changes, and this brought new people and places around me. I accepted to earn less money whilst I made changes, and I accepted this way of living, a way that allowed me to give effortlessly. It was a life I really wanted, and I let go of opportunities that contradicted this.

In return, I have received the best health. My body is relaxed, and my mind takes mini-breaks. Life is not a constant smile; however, it can be constant love in your heart, and this love creates all the effortless giving you have to offer.

Each of us is an individual with our own priorities on our own personal journey. I've chosen to share parts of my journey with you, and this is not to say the same is right for you, (but it is right for me, right now). The lesson is about our alignment with internal love. When we act out and live through our hearts, our mental and physical bodies are aligned, which gives us health.

One of my priorities after I came back to being Emma after an encounter with depression, (I wanted to write *my encounter*; however, I removed *my* because that creates ownership of the depression, and I don't own it) was to stand on a table in an office where I knew of other people, colleagues who were going through the same thing or living with anxiety attacks and the physical effects of stress, and shout out that there was nothing to be ashamed of and to share my experiences and of the help and support I received from friends (who I did not know where friends.) Instead, I'm going to stand on the Great Wall of China and shout it from there!

One of the biggest disappointments and misunderstandings many people have of when they have helped others, is when they need support for themselves, and they find their 'friends' do not help. This is important for us to learn and accept it is not that our friends have stopped loving us. Instead look at it as there are other people who we might not have met before who can help us with what we are going through. Allow yourself always to accept new friendship, as this is a gift to you; with play, love and learning.

Remember as you stand on your stage with your stage light bright above you that there are many other dancing lights, and these are your friends. Some shine brighter right now, and as the scene develops, the lights change and the dance continues.

Enjoy giving effortlessly from your heart with love, allowing you to grow your love of your life today, tomorrow, and every day.

be giving. be grateful. be accepting. be learning. be loving. be life. be happy. belifehappy.

Play: And Capture

· ·

2 June 2010

We enter this world with all forms of play around us, and in fact, most of the play is learning. As we progress through our years, play continues with learning and developing the beliefs and values we associate with areas in our lives. As we start working and take on daily responsibilities, play becomes less, and we learn less. At times, we feel less playful.

When we allow the time to play, we bring back the power of learning into our lives for that experience. The learning helps us grow individually, helps maintain our balance in mind and body, and allows us happiness and joy.

Play is anything that brings joy, and most of all, this describes capturing and recording moments of happiness. Photography is something everyone has access to. It is how we perceive our surroundings. We have the ability to learn through our images. What and why a photograph was captured can help us understand and see what our world looks like in the very moment the photograph was taken.

Whether you capture the bright colours of the flowers in your garden, people, buildings while walking, or happy times with family and friends, the smiles, vibrancy, and feelings of what you see will show you how you perceive the object you are capturing.

Photography is art. It is something you can learn and master with different techniques. It allows challenges of mental skill, patience, creativity, and flexibility. What do you want this image to look like? What would happen if you changed your focus? Adjusted your angle? Perhaps moved closer to the subject? What would happen if you added more light? How would the photograph feel in black and white? These questions are similar to what we can ask ourselves daily when we look around us. Do you see the vibrancy of the green of the trees? The brightness and warmth from flowers in your garden?

You have the same control on the result of your photography as you do in your life. To make changes to the image, close your eyes and create the image. Feel, touch, hear, and taste it, and when you open your eyes, what do you see?

Photography creates a stillness of the mind through focus on an object or moment. This stillness allows the mind and body to relax and be in the present moment, enjoying and playing.

Let's turn up the brightness in your day and play today, tomorrow, and every day. belifehappy.

Love: Relationships Versus You

. . . .

3 June 2010

Butterflies carry on their wings eternal love for you today, tomorrow, and every day.

After recently watching the first *Sex and the City* movie, I was drawn to how when Carrie interviews candidates to be her personal assistant, it is Jennifer Hudson's character's answer of moving to the Big Apple to find love that catches Carrie's attention. My ears perked up, and I immediately thought of how different love was in a relationship to that of love for yourself. The sequel is out, and I've not yet seen it, so I don't have any answers from the film. I do, however, have some questions about this! So here we go on relationships versus love.

Relationships: The search is on

When we decide we want to meet a partner, we are tuned into this frequency. We often get a little disappointed when it doesn't quite turn out the way we'd expect, though. "Confident, feeling good," says the angel on your left shoulder, and in your right ear you hear yourself say, "I really want to meet someone because I don't want to be on my own anymore."

Meeting the one (you might have already!)

You meet, and you're in love, your world spins. All you see is love in everything. The flutter of your energy mixing leaves you feeling amazing, like you are dancing on air. For each moment, you are special, and you are loved.

Time goes by

The sparkles and pizazz calm down, and daily life returns. You start to notice the grey clouds on the way to work, and the traffic queue once again irritates you. You feel like you are missing something and yet don't know. All these emotions go home with you, inside you, and now and again you erupt with a few words. You feel better for the release.

When it comes to an end (as some love stories go)

Torn and broken: That's your heart. You feel ill, and the light has darkened. You feel alone and lonely. After the hurt, you begin to question why this happened to you. How will you ever find the right one?

Love: The search is on

You asked the question why and waited and waited and waited patiently, and the answers started to come. With each answer you were given, you started to question more. Eventually, a different feeling starts to emerge about you and your world.

Meeting the one (well, it's all individual)

Meeting with your love, your pure source of energy, is the greatest mind-blowing experience. It's unexplainable to others, a feeling of immense pure and unconditional love. A release and acceptance of all you are and all you are part of. For that moment and future moments, love becomes the greatest friend, greatest inspiration, greatest creativity, and greatest love.

Time goes by

After the learning of this beautiful source of energy is reached, daily life continues, except you become more aware of daily life and how you play a role in your day. How you direct your day. You remember the ultimate feeling of love and are able to make choices you once procrastinated about. You continue to learn each day from everything and everyone around you. You start your day welcoming love and end it with gratitude for the love in your day. You know you are not alone, and feeling lonely is an emotion you have replaced with your complete acceptance and love of yourself.

When it comes to an end (as some love stories do)

When you find this love, it is unconditional and eternal. You have this love for your lifetime. You can stop loving yourself at any time through choice. Why would you? When you love you, your world loves you.

So what is there to learn about relationships versus love? Relationships can leave us, and while we had the feelings of love, these have an opposite of emptiness and loss, which we ultimately feel when we say goodbye to someone we love. With love from our own source, our dependency on love is already fulfilled and therefore removes the desperate feeling of needing to be in love.

Falling in love with ourselves is the searching and meeting who we really are and being truthful with what we believe and feel is our true purpose. With this, we begin to make decisions for ourselves that match our beliefs and feelings. All of our cells sing, sing, sing loudly of love and joy.

How to find someone who has found love

It's the same as when you see one of your friends who is in a new relationship. You see the sparkles of light in their eyes. They walk like they are secretly dancing (on air) and smile. These are just for starters. It is not disappointing, however, to meet someone who has found love to not smile because some days are learning days!

Find, give, play, love, and learn in love. Whether you prefer to be in love in a relationship or in love with yourself and single or in a relationship is your choice. Love is your gift which you allow for yourself. Stay open to love, and let its frequency flow through you today, tomorrow, and every day.

be love. be life. be happy.

Release Your Entertainer

· ·

7 June 2010

The last seventy-two hours have had me spinning around, from seeing the Pope in Cyprus when he visited Paphos, to reclaiming my youth at a club night and also meeting lots of new and interesting people. Only last Thursday, I was feeling a little lost. Being blessed with some very inspirational friends, one reminded me to focus the day on abundance. I did: Abundance in all areas of my life, and the following days transformed with joyful emotions and people.

All individuals who place themselves in the public realm (yes, even you with your Facebook profile) is entertaining an audience in some way, and this is what transpired for me this weekend. Whilst my visit to see the Pope was one of historical value rather than of religion, I had still unconsciously set a level of expectation of actually seeing him. Whether it was a spiritual expectation as we all believe, I am not sure. My body, however, spoke for me in taking my hand, which I realised minutes later had been held against my stomach and my solar plexus, and I felt sick. Asking myself why this experience would create a feeling of nausea, I came to the conclusion that it was emotional disappointment of not being able to hear him properly as I was quite far back. My level of expectation hadn't been met. There are several explanations of the solar plexus chakra, and my simple translation is of one of our body's main power houses of emotion and intuition. Personally, I'm not clear on why I felt this on seeing the Pope, and I imagine it will come to light when I'm ready to understand.

I moved from the feeling of nausea to complete opposite emotions created by another entertainer, this time in the form of a DJ. The club scene is not somewhere you would be likely to find me anymore. I still love dancing, and this was no exception! This DJ was creating a room full of happiness: What an awesome gift! This was the first time I had ever thought of a DJ in this way. Before I figured DJs just played and mixed records, right? Now there was a whole experience, feelings and emotions that were being created by this one person.

These two events and polar-opposite individuals sparked in my mind about how we are each entertainers within our universe and to our audience. This can be our audience at home with our family, at work with our colleagues, or with friends socially. The questions that naturally follow are:

How do you create and entertain in your day?

What atmosphere and emotions do you project outwardly into your universe?

It starts within us as the creation, so on reflection what I was feeling inside about the events I attended was first disappointment of not receiving my full experience, and then secondly complete happiness, with feelings of joyful expression to be able to be in the moment of music and dance. My experiences of each event will also be very different from others who attended. That is the true uniqueness of who we are in that we create our experience. What could I have done to improve my first experience? I could have researched and found out how I got a pass to stand closer. That's really how simple it is.

From enjoying the experiences of the entertainers in our worlds, remember you are an entertainer, too. What experience do you want to create for your audience today, tomorrow, and every day? Ask what action, if any, you need to make to create the brightest experience? Stand forward, take control, and turn up the brightness in your universe!

Give: Thanks

8 June 2010

Attitude of gratitude. Three words can change your day today, tomorrow, and every day. It's simple and frequently forgotten how the act of giving thanks throughout our day can create a happier you.

We can be a little shortsighted in our gratitude and be thankful for only significant things in our life. This is where extending our vision is often helpful. We close our eyes and are still, and when we open our eyes, we see so much more. We have so much more to be thankful for!

Some families give thanks for their food on the table, I remember doing this as a child. Now life is much more demanding, and while I give thanks for my day, I no longer give thanks before I eat. Dinner for one at home has become, at times, simply a necessary function.

The basis of the attitude of gratitude is that we practice like everything on this journey. What we do today will change tomorrow, and when you stop, so do the changes. It is an ongoing daily progress of being thankful.

When was the last time you sat and wrote a list of what you are thankful in your life? And secondly, why would you? It's really not something we would place on the top of our daily priority list. To give yourself five minutes to write this list while on your coffee break, whilst watching TV, or before you go to bed, you not only give thanks for your life, but you also give acceptance and release what you are thankful for.

As we hold on to things, we become cluttered, except we're not really talking about material clutter here. Rather, it's more emotional clutter. Clutter creates blockages, similar to a traffic jam on a highway, and we all know a traffic jam is not great. How does it make you feel? A little anxious and angry maybe? And with each bit of clutter, you create more of these negative emotions, leading to a general unhappiness.

Can being thankful and adopting this attitude of gratitude really make a difference? It really does by simplifying what is in your life in the present moment. It also helps you identify very quickly what you have in your life that perhaps you are not thankful for. That being the case, you can ask yourself why it is in your life. Your list can be endless, or you can create a focused list on key areas of your life and all the things you are thankful for in that specific area. Again, it's a great way to review and declutter!

Your list is your list, because it represents what is in your world and what you are thankful for. Whilst washing up, I realised I was thankful for the day I had experienced so far. From that, I realised I was thankful for the great network of people in my life, and by being thankful, I was accepting these experiences.

I am receiving, and I am grateful to receive. I am now in control of these experiences, and my direction of thought will direct the outcomes.

(What a responsibility we have to ourselves!)

The attitude of gratitude allows free-flowing experiences in your life, moment by moment. Saying yes, accepting the experience, and being thankful for the experience continues the flow through you. I can hear someone asking, "That's OK, however, how am I going to be thankful for being stuck in a traffic jam and being late for an appointment?" When you are in the traffic jam, ask how can you change the situation? Unless there is a detour, the main thing you can do is call ahead (hands-free, of course) of your appointment. Your courtesy will be thanked, and the rest of your day will continue in the flow. You will not add to your emotional clutter, which in turn keeps you calmer.

Start now, and let your attitude of gratitude flow freely today, tomorrow, and every day.

Play: Discover Your ZING (Zone. In. Now. Go!)

· ·

9 June 2010

Joy is an unconditional emotion, something that fills us with happiness, and whilst at times we experience this emotion for only a brief moment, by discovering and experiencing new activities of play in our day, we can create more of these brief moments of unconditional joy.

These emotions are amazing for us in mind, body, and spirit. These brief moments will have you dancing, singing, smiling, laughing, and experiencing inner peace and love of pure unconditional beauty. This will have every cell beaming light! Imagine your body right now with lots of lines (arteries and veins) that are now bright white light pulsing upwards through your entire body, racing with joy and love and exploding through the top of your head, the palms of your hands, and the soles of your feet. You become your light, a stunning, awesome, shinning beacon of joy. Do you feel it? Are you seeing it right now? ZING! (zone. in. now. go!)

What will we do to create the ZING? Let's look at the zone. What creates a zone? It's a place and space in time which you have created, that leads to now. Where do you go when you are in your zone? You will find your now, and within your now, you can go! Go and create, be you, be alive, be ZING, and belifehappy!

Discovering your zone is not always as easy as it first sounds, although it will be when you find it. We all try different activities for a brief time, and we give up simply because we tried. To find your Zone, the first thing you must do is to stop trying and start experiencing! That means to remove your limits. You do not have to go to the gym or do one or two forms of activity. What would happen if you experienced something new, like a different activity? Does this sound crazy?

If you always go to the gym, you will only experience the zone you create in the gym. If you were to go to the gym and then go for a walk, you would start to experience another zone. These are similar regular activities. To create more ZING in your day, there are other things you can do, be and have; maybe just once to simply have the experience. Do you and a friend, partner, or family member have different play activities, such as:

Mum is a photographer, and son mountain bikes?
Husband plays golf, and wife swims and does spinning classes?
Friend goes hiking, and another friend goes to the theatre?
Dad listens to classical music, and daughter goes salsa dancing?

These are random suggestions and all potentially realistic. Why not find out now about experiencing someone else's ZING experience? Say yes to a new ZING! Discover a new zone, get in the now, and enjoy the flow of zing! Say yes this time, and next time in your play time, you can choose what you would like to do to discover your zone. Outdoor activities including walking, cycling, and golf; learning an art, like painting or photography; relaxation, through meditation and yoga and holistic therapy; and visiting new places with new scenery and beauty to capture and music to inspire or learn a new dance are all possibilities. Life presents us with many ZINGs, and we have the choice of how many brief moments of ZING we want to experience. I'm not suggesting living in a constant state of ZING! Rather, just to allow yourself to discover ways to have more experiences than just a few brief moments for our mind, body, and spirit to light up our worlds and shine brightly. ZING!

be ZING. be joy. be life. be happy. belifehappy.

Love: Free-flowing

• •

10 June 2010

Our ideal is to be a free-flowing highway traveling north and south, the outward journey breathing in the new and the return journey collecting waste materials, recycling, and exhaling the old. Our mind and body work together, and what we leave behind physically affects the mind. What we hold on to mentally affects the body. To achieve the ideal free-flowing highway, we can do simple things to release physical waste and look at new techniques for emotional release. Everything to help restore and maintain balance today, tomorrow, and every day.

Physically, part of our job is to release the waste materials to prevent a build-up traffic jam, and this is where drinking water and moderate exercise (from walking the dog, walking to the shops, and taking the stairs not the lift) helps in working the systems in our bodies to release the toxins. (Note the use of the word *toxins*; maybe you want to help start removing them!)

Staying with our physiology, breathing also helps our bodies release waste materials. Often, small changes in our breathing and posture will improve our mind and body. When we are running around every day, we will find our breathing is shallower and more frequent, taking in oxygen to fuel our fast-paced life. For those of us who sit during the day, if our posture is out of alignment, the air we breathe in and exhale is not as free-flowing. Therefore, it is not as effective, whereas this technique below will help you improve your breathing at the start and end of your day.

Exercise

Sit on a chair with your back straight and head high. Place your left hand over your heart and your right hand over your stomach, and close your eyes. As you breathe in, notice the movement of your stomach. Now take a deep breath in, and exhale feeling as though you are flushing your body with new light. Hold it, and now exhale slowly and intentionally. Release your breath out there, and release everything you want to let go of. Exhale until it has all left you, breathe in, and repeat up to five times. On your last breath, take your hands away from your body and shake them at your sides. As you exhale, slowly open your eyes and then return to your regular breathing. Look around the room, and when you are wide awake, you are ready to go.

This type of exercise can be done anywhere. When you are feeling under pressure, this technique will help you calm and centre yourself and relax your body and mind.

Physically, we know breathing and any moderate exercise will help with our free-flowing highway. There are other road blocks that occur through our mind creation which can lead to disease. To help remove and manage these problems, we can – just like with our physical bodies – apply a few techniques to help us.

Emotional clutter is something we can miss very easily as we cannot see or feel it as clearly; however, when we have too much, our physical bodies will often send us warning signs. We have a filter in our minds to process the enormous amount of information we come across in our day. The filter allows you to see what you want to see; feel what you want to feel; and hear what you want to hear, touch, and taste. We create beliefs, values, and attitudes, and these act as our filter. We also operate on a level where when we feel hurt by something someone has said or done or not done, this feeling will attach itself to an area in the filing system. It joins a queue of other key emotions: anger, sadness, fear, hurt, and guilt. Without acknowledging, accepting, and releasing each emotion we experience, we create a traffic queue. This highway is endless. It will keep adding to each queue, and when a similar situation occurs to one of your unresolved emotions, it will, like a car junkyard, pick up the emotion and throw it right there in front of your eyes! It is up to you how you manage it. Will you ignore or release it?

Without releasing our emotions, our bodies respond with physical warnings (aches and pains, painful backs caused by tension, headaches, nausea, and IBS). We can become scared of facing our emotions and continue to carry these around with us, and carry we do! Our bodies reflect the weight through exhaustion, slumped shoulders, and lack of interest, and the future stops on the highway look more like anxiety attacks, panic attacks, and depression.

For some of us, we do not see or feel the warning signs, and the point here is to create things in our day so we can actively choose to release the emotions as we go along. We can do this with gratitude, giving thanks when we wake up and at the end of the day and allowing acceptance of everything in your day. Any form of time you spend on yourself, you can use this time to acknowledge things that upset us and accept and release them.

You can decide how you wish to manage every emotion. Likewise, if you wish to hold on to an emotion, you can, and you can also ask how this will help you flow freely.

For now, spend time on your highway, help it become free-flowing and relaxed, check your pace and balance, look out for warning signs, and give thanks every day.

be love. be life. be happy.

Just a Nudge

. . . .

14 June 2010

Yesterday, I found the goals I had written in pencil on 14 January 2010, six months ago. The goals were personal, including releasing limiting beliefs I'd had on a specific area in my life.

2009 was a roller coaster year: nonstop study, learning, practice, and more learning. Then, there was the breakthrough nearly twelve months ago when I was trained to become an NLP practitioner and coach. To do this, you experience all of the training, and there was my breakthrough and another move (to another country, no less).

Whilst I have achieved all my goals, for the last few weeks, I have felt some unease and not really had any answers. (This means I did! I just didn't want to admit to really knowing!) Finding my goals was not by chance. I'm more than sure they were placed in front of me to say, "Update me, please" with sirens and great big flashing lights. I feel pretty fulfilled in my life in this moment (and I say *pretty fulfilled* based on the fact I still let my mind and other people's reality affect me to an extent). Years ago, I would spend my days wishing and wanting anything but the life I was living. Thank goodness I changed it. Now I have no wishes and no wants. However, I still create goals, and these goals are in alignment with what I believe my purpose is: to help other people restore and maintain balance in their lives through coaching and holistic therapies. This is my giving in life – to help support and raise the consciousness levels to a higher vibration of love, compassion, joy, and peace through what I love: communication.

In play, I am more active than ever before through walking and training for the charity trek I am doing the Mental Health Foundation and getting on my bike after nearly six years. Yesterday, I got back in the pool and have a good few months of swimming to get on with. My shelves are full of inspiring books, and my iPod is to capacity with music I once would not of dreamed of listening to (classical - now love it!). I've been to see the Pope, and I've partied with an old school house DJ in the same week!

In love, I am blessed with wonderful friends, family, and belifehappy friends who bring so much joy in to my life every day! Love brings lessons every day in the beauty around us, and when the beauty fades or even disappears, it is knowing how to recognise this and how to bring it back by finding your ZING!

Learning comes moment by moment, as well as in spells where I have discovered by a little retreat that I can gather my thoughts, process, and move on. I have learned by reading new books and from different spiritual teachers, as well as by finding friends who have the same interests and learning from them. So far, it has been six months of expanse – a night sky being filled with so many shinning bright stars, creating a galaxy of uplifting consciousness – and I am so blessed to be learning with you.

So what happens now? It's all about balance. In giving, my aim is to grow and continue sharing my experiences and other enlightening inspirational people's experiences with you. In play, I'm leaving the doors open as this has led me to so many places I have not been before. No limits in play! In love, my aim is to continue to change, accept, believe, and trust in my mind, body, and spirit. I am loving my internal world to be able to share this love with the universe. The learning is my life. Without it, I stop inside. It is my adventure, play, inspiration, and love. I learn from meeting new people, catching up with old friends, walking along the coast, and even watching Twitter updates. Everywhere I go with open eyes and I learn.

Whilst I have shared with you my aims, I know I need to create my list and place it back inside the cupboard, so when the end of the year comes, I will check back on it. The feeling right now is to go and create! The universe of which we are all collectively a part of is awesomely amazing. To feel, see, and hear it, we just have to listen to ourselves, believe we can do it, and start being it. Go create!

With love and light sparkle smiles always fluttering at your side today, tomorrow, and every day.

Give: Time

· ·

15 June 2010

This chapter title is actually a contradiction. How can we give time when time is relative, and who, what, where, is time relative too? Panic! Have we just lost time in this moment? Surely not as we are both in this time right now, aren't we? Time is still here; it's just a perspective on which time we are in. Are you in your time, are you in my time, or are we both actually in someone else's time?

I'm still here! Are you? Then we must be in the same time. Let's find out how time really does influence giving in your world. Time is often something we worry about we are running out of. Are you running out of time? Time is in our worlds. Regardless of where we live on this planet, time has an influence on us. We're going to still be sleeping the recommended six to eight hours a night, waking in the morning, and working or filling our days with what we do by time because we all live by time.

I believe some people do live in their own time, and whilst this still works with the universal time, the universal time and the individual's time are in flow and therefore a happiness of time. When we live in only the external universe's time, we have in effect lost our own individual time and we are not in the flow. We feel constantly pushed for time and out of time, and in this universe, we simply have no time to give to ourselves, let alone to anyone else who might need our help.

Again, when we live outside of the flow of time, our body and mind become affected by the imbalance. We might experience anger, resentment, anxiety, tension, and high levels of stress. This is all from simply being out of the flow of time.

So is there a river that time flows through or a big universal clock we climb to the top of and then jump into the river of time and constantly flow down? Not that I have found or heard of, although doesn't that sound fun? Within ourselves, however, we do have the ability to create our own time.

To change your time, look at the areas in your life where time is something you are short on. Do you run late for work? Not have enough time for the project or for meeting deadlines? For lunch? No time to get to the gym, walk the dog, get to the Tuesday yoga class? No time to prepare a meal or no time for you and your partner to spend time together? Look at everything, and examine the times where you experience stress or anger. When you have identified where your time is out of balance, you can jump back in the flow.

We all have enough time. Your colleague has the same amount of universal time as you, as does your friend who goes to the gym three times a week. It really does come down to how you would like to spend and manage your time. When we live in fear of not having enough time to ultimately survive, we panic and get stressed and anxious. What would happen if you were to say and affirm to yourself, "I am time?" Nothing? Okay. When you accept time, and each moment of time is what you create, you become your own time, which is in flow with universal time.

The more you remind yourself that time is not to be feared, you are allowing yourself to have abundant time. It works only when you believe it. When you are in the flow of universal time, you will know what time it is because of how you feel, not by looking a watch.

I have an abundance of time in my day to achieve: (fill in).

When you control time, you are in time. When time controls you, you are out of time.

Give yourself time, and allow and accept time to be you. You always have time to do what you want in every moment. Keep your flow of thoughts on what and where you want to be, and you will align yourself in time. If you continue to fight against time, you will be late and feel rushed and under pressure.

Time is a friend waiting at the top of the hill, ready to take your hand so you can roll together.

be giving. be balance. be time. be flowing. be joyful. be love. be life. be happy. belifehappy.

Play: Improve Your Game?

. . . .

16 June 2010

We're not talking about any particular game, and when I talked about giving time, as many of us feel up against the clock most days, play moves out of the way for daily routine. (I don't like the word *routine*: Let's change that to *daily tasks*!) Finding time to bring play into our days is not always up to the clock. Many of us use excuses not to play, and this includes not having enough time to something in the house that needs doing; the food shopping needs to be done; or the ironing, cleaning the windows, washing your hair (now we reach the extreme of excuses!) needs to be taken care of.

When we make an excuse for not doing something we agreed to experience, it is just that: an excuse. Why do we make excuses? The honest answer is that we don't actually want to do the activity we have excused ourselves from.

We work like a cog wheel, two cogs turning into each other. This is our mind and body. They continually turn in alignment with our internal beliefs and values. When the mind or body wants to do something that is not in alignment with your internal beliefs and values, the cogs slip. Our response is to make an excuse. The cog slipping is similar to the feeling of anxiety, or if that is not recognised, a general feeling of unease about doing something arises. How often do you do things you don't feel great about doing and then give up because you don't feel you are very good at it?

This happens for most people, and we still make excuses for why we are no longer going to the gym (and still paying the membership), why we haven't got round to reading the new books we've ordered, why the plants bought at the garden centre are still in their pots, (surviving!), and why the new mountain bike has been out of the garage only once. The question you can ask yourself when you are no longer interested in your play is, "is this activity in alignment with my values and beliefs?" In fact, most of us would not clearly know what our values are about an activity until we are asked. Our values and beliefs are formed by our childhood, family members, friends, and colleagues, and whilst our values and beliefs change over time, would you recognise the values you have placed in your life regarding relaxation, health, fitness, well-being, career, relationships, and play?

Many times, we can easily say, "I can't do that, I'm not good enough." Immediately, we have limited ourselves against the opportunity to be good at whatever it was. Over time, we can believe we are not good enough, which limits us in the future.

Have you started thinking about your play and your values and beliefs about it? Are you limiting yourself against opportunities to expand play in your day?

Sometimes, all we require is a little outside support to understand how we can improve our play. This can be as simple as identifying where your values are and how your prioritise them, and you will see in black and white the why. With a little more support, you can release those limiting beliefs and fly into your day with play.

Play is a free flow of joy. There is no uneasy feeling. Instead, you welcome achievement, excitement, confidence, and relaxation. You, all of us, have the ability to unlock the door to our values and beliefs and reassess honestly what we want to experience. When you do this, the 'how' just happens.

Doing it on our own is possible; however, you'll find great NLP coaches who will work with you on this over a few sessions. You are the resource: The coach simply holds your hand, and watches as you align yourself with you.

Know your universe is filled with inspiration, creativity, joy, and love through play. Know your goals, align your cogs, and go!

be honest. be inspired. be creative. be joy. be love. be life. be happy. belifehappy.

Champion Time

. . . .

21 June 2010

Welcome to another wonderful new day. These last few weeks have been quite a roller coaster ride, with old and new friends coming in and out. With each meeting, there is a new lesson. I wanted to talk to you about champions. I realised, though, that I've been writing a lot about champions for a client of mine recently, and I discovered it was people champions I want to share with you.

People champions are friends who are not always there every day, and you may hear from them only once in a while, but all the time, they are championing you, believing in you, and sending you love. Each champion is a gift. My champion is awesome. She doesn't use the Internet, will not read this for maybe a year or so, and has known me since I was eleven. As she said, I will always be the Emma in the school photo we had taken when we were fourteen years old! This lady is not always there physically; however, in mind and in heart, I know she is thinking of me as I do her.

The other thing I want to share is space. Thinking space – or really, nonthinking space – is what I mean. It has been difficult for me to get in that space for a few weeks, and as a result, I have become very tired and halted my usual action focus. This weekend, I spent some me time, and strangely, this found me working for a few hours on a very mundane job, which gave me the opportunity for some nonthinking space. In that time, I found some inspiration for a creative project I'm working on and generally switched off. Yesterday, I continued the theme reading, and I did a lovely self-healing treatment, after which I felt very refreshed.

Finding our ZING really does work! Whether we are being paid or it is an activity we enjoy, we can and need to sometimes allow and create the nonthinking space so we can ZING!

Times are changing. A new or maybe a more defined vision is appearing, and as I discovered with my champion, I have been fighting this for a few weeks, being me is much more beautiful. It took me years to understand it, and (with a smile as I write), I am in love with myself.

It's always good to experience places and new people; however, when they repeat old patterns that didn't create happiness, why repeat them? That's what I had been fighting against. We're not responsible for other people's lives. We are responsible for our own. When I am not happy, I will always choose to change the situation. That's the biggest lesson I have learned. I believe I experienced a test of what was and how I would approach it now. And the journey continues.

be a champion. be championing. be ZING. be inspiring. be creative. be love.

Give: It's Your World

22 June 2010

Give. That's what we have to do. Giving is a good thing.

Whilst fluttering through our days, I heard this comment, "Giving is good it is part of our balance ..." It's part of the balance of the all, the *all* being your universe.

Separation is no longer. We are one, and therefore, when we are separate, it becomes easier to disassociate with the balance. In effect, we can ignore it until the imbalance gets your attention.

Our ego is a disassociation of the universe, a place where we allow fear and negative emotions (such as anger, sadness, fear, hurt, and guilt) to hold and limit us from the free flow of the universe. We hold back from giving for fear of losing what we have. In times where there is instability in the world around us, we can let that instability become part of our lives, and we fight to hold on to everything we have. Some people, and we have all seen this, are always giving. They give their time, kindness, support, and love. The imbalance? They do not allow themselves to receive help, support, and love.

Some of the happiest times are times of instability when groups of friends and families begin to share support, kindness, and love. Do you remember those times? The instability can be in times of external influences. Think of the strength of our grandparents during the war. Think about when within your family, there is illness or bereavement. Everyone flicks a switch for support, kindness, and love. Why do we wait for difficult times to be in balance?

Simple acts of giving ensure you remain in balance with receiving. Breathe in, receive the oxygen, and fill your body with energy. Exhale, and let go of your fears and limits.

Give your gifts to help others, and be open to receiving more gifts.

Allow yourself to give. Share your knowledge and experiences, and look around: Are there people in your world who have asked for your help? Or perhaps you know that they would like some help? Give them a call, or pay them visit. Giving of your time could potentially change their day. The universe is all. You are the universe. You are responsible for your universe and its balance.

Allow yourself to receive. Allow time to relax: You deserve that! Receive openly the help offered to you. Life is not meant to be a struggle (a lesson learned from another dear teacher and friend.) Let's stop our fight, and free flow! Go! Yay!

be giving. be receiving. be balance. be love. be life. be happy. belifehappy.

Play: Movies to Inspire

. . . .

23 June 2010

See it. Feel it. Hear it. Understand it?

Movies are an awesome source of creativity. It's time we allow ourselves to become emerged in someone else's world, even more so now with the technology of surround sound. Then add in HD TVs with their super-sharp sound and vision. Are you seeing it? Feeling it? Hearing it? Understanding it?

Having recently watched the movie *Avatar* as a recommendation from a friend, I found that although my TV is not supersonic, as the movie progressed, I felt the sound dance around my living room and the light from the screen flow all around. For me, it was like magic. What we take away from a movie or any experience is individual, and whilst the movie had great tones of greed, anger, and destruction – all very negative emotions – for me, the movie was a learning experience that I really enjoyed.

These quotes below were taken from throughout the movie that inspired me;

"The tree of voices is inside of you."
"All energy is borrowed, one day you have to give it back."
"Your thoughts control and seal your next move..."
"Shut up and fly straight!"

These quotes defined a personal view of the universe and how we have all the resources to discover our purpose and answers and how our thoughts are more powerful than we believe until we are in a situation when our thoughts are present. They are most powerful because of their focus and intention. The quote touching my soul was, "I see you." To me, that said much more than "I love you" because they were seeing into each other's souls. This is love, the pure divine source.

The movie embraced fear, and the following two quotes I wrote from my own learning;

"When you are afraid you let in anger. When you are joyful you embrace love."

"Greed - interfering in someone's universe, because you are unfulfilled with your own."

And finally, I leave you with in my own words;

The universe we are all one hand from another. We share.
Follow the light and trust where it guides you.
Trust you are connected to a source.
The people are one, one source connected. The universe is inside you.

be joy. be inspired. be creative. be seeing. be feeling. be hearing. be love. be life. be happy. belifehappy.

Love: Relaxing Your Mind and Body

. . . .

24 June 2010

Creating the space and time to relax helps your mind and body relax, allowing you to be fully in the moment and enjoy your work, relationships, health, fitness, and finances. When you are relaxed, you are in control.

Use this simple relaxation to help you now relax for ten minutes. Enjoy!

Exercise

Relax now, peacefully and within yourself. Find a space where you can be yourself. Now, rest and relax your body, starting with your breathing.

Place your left hand over your heart and your right hand just below your belly button. As you breathe in, focus your attention on drawing your breath down your spine and into your stomach. As you inhale, feel your stomach rise. Exhale slowly through your mouth, feeling the air releasing from your tummy, cleansing all your vital organs, and expelling your worries and tension.

Let's do this three more of these. Now inhale slowly, feel the air flushing your body, and exhale. Let go, let go, and release your tension.

Feel your body begin to relax and feel heavier as you inhale slowly, feeling your scalp, face, and neck all relaxing, reaching the air into your tummy. Exhale slowly as you feel the negative energy leaving your body. Feel your shoulders, arms, and hands relax.

As you breathe in, feel you spine sink into your chair as each vertebrae relaxes, feel your stomach relax, and now feel your pelvis relax. You begin to feel heavier and more relaxed as you exhale, relaxing your thighs, knees, and calf muscles. Relax your ankles and feet through to your toes. Relax now.

Keep your attention on your breathing, and see the wonderful meadow you are standing in. You are perfectly safe in this calm meadow. Listen to my voice. I am here with you, guiding you through the beauty of this natural piece of paradise.

Now, take off your shoes and socks and walk barefoot on the beautiful, rich green grass. Feel the grass tickle your toes. Wriggle your toes in the grass. You are smiling, and you feel more relaxed.

The light from the yellow sunshine radiates warmth and happiness all around you, from your head to your toes. Warmth and happiness. Under your feet, the green grass offers you security and love connecting you to nature.

In the distance, you hear birds singing in the trees of a forest just ahead. You follow the calming birdsong and reach the entrance of the forest. Feel the energy of the trees, and hear the breeze whispering through the leaves. See the brightness of the colours. For this moment, you are the forest. It talks to you, and you feel safe and relaxed.

Just ahead, a tree has fallen with a seat carved into it. The seat is inviting and shiny and smooth, light oak. Touch the wood, and feel its richness and smoothness. Sit down and relax.

As you relax into this seat, enjoy the sounds, smells, colours, and feelings of peace from this forest. Enjoy this feeling for a few moments. Relax and feel safe in this enriching forest. Listen to the birds. Observe nature. Feel.

What beautiful sounds, what beautiful peace. You are now ready to leave this forest and go back to the meadow, knowing you can come here and sit peacefully whenever you want to. Begin your walk slowly back to the meadow. Start to feel the movement of your tummy as you breathe. See the blue sky now as you approach the meadow. Start to become aware of your body or your fingers and toes. Count with me from one to five. One, wiggle your toes. Two, become aware of your breathing. Three, become aware of the room. Four, start to open your eyes. Five, you're wide awake and back in the room now.

Return to regular breathing, and have a glass of water.

Love yourself. Your mind and body. belifehappy. x

Respect Each Other's Model of the World

. . . .

28 June 2010

Fear, ego, and respect. These three words interlink, and they have been part of my learning in the last week. Our ego creates fear; it is our naysayer in life, the one we allow to limit us by calling out, "Well you've failed. You can't possibly do that. You're not good enough."

I was asked just the other day how someone who owns a website called belifehappy could be not ultimately happy? What was their perception of happiness? And was it the same as mine? My answer was, "In my heart I am very happy, I believe in what I do, how I do it and enjoy it. I am learning just as everyone who chooses to learn, and as we grow, we face unresolved parts of the past and I could ignore them bury them away ... but they will only come back... and this time round, I am choosing to face them, learn, and move on... and that isn't as easy as I thought."

My own belief: "A bank balance does not indicate success or failure. Your heart is the richest asset we each own. For that, I feel very rich and thankful."

Respect each other's models of the world. We all have individual values and beliefs. A person who chooses to make profit and a person who lives to live: It comes down to respect. Neither individual is greater than the other; they simply live with different beliefs and values. At some point in their lifetime, they might meet and find they have a hobby or interest in common, and all the preconceived ideas of each other float away.

Respect and support people around you, and when something is in your life that no longer bears meaning, adds value, or presents a positive, remove it. Don't let fear take over. You have all the resources, and when you let go of what is not good for you, more good rushes in. I feel the fear as I grow and learn. We can at times get carried away with it and are helped often by the people around us, who also let their egos fear come out to play. The way to leave the ego is to learn to question our feelings and turn each situation around to be positive.

There is no prize for the person who reaches the finish line with the most money and assets.

Today is simply for being happy, balanced, loving, and kind. When life is out of balance, you have control to reclaim the balance. And if you choose to remain the same, accept this is how it is.

Over the next month, I am personally planning on reclaiming balance in my life as I've not allowed time for growth as it has been a very busy time with two house moves and lots of trek training. My growth is my light and energy, and I share this with you.

Think about how you respect the people in your life, their view of the world, and how they respect yours. Simply listening, seeing, and feeling the other perspective allows us to understand, accept, and respect.

be respectful. be supportive. be kind. be love. be life. be happy. belifehappy.

Give: Challenges

. . . .

29 June 2010

Feelings of boredom, agitation, and frustration come from not being stimulated, either physically or mentally, and we often don't see this. When we are so busy and when our minds are busy with things that we have allowed to worry us, we simply don't have the time to stimulate and challenge ourselves. The results, though, will be seen and felt in your confidence, self-esteem, and general well-being.

A challenge sounds like you have to go and do something really big, and it doesn't have to be. A challenge is anything, mental or physical, that pushes your boundaries: According to the Oxford Mini Dictionary, it is to "Call to try one's skill or strength."

Physical challenges test our learning and skill, physical strength, and stamina: walking, cycling, running, jogging, swimming, tennis, golf, and horse riding, for example. The endorphins don't take long for us to start to want to do the activity again and again. Enjoy the activity and push ourselves sensibly. The only person in the race is you, so ultimately, you are the only one to receive the rewards.

Our mental stimulation is through learning and skill, showing greater knowledge, and this is limitless. Personal development is mental stimulation, reading acclaimed authors, spiritual teachers, and learning how to maintain balance in our mind and bodies. Other activities, for example, include baking, floristry, painting, drawing, pottery, needlework, language classes, crossword puzzles, and

Sudoku. And when you have learned one level and enjoy it, you then can continue to progress. There is always somewhere to continue to.

By giving yourself a challenge, the benefits far outweigh the let's leave it for another day! Through learning a new activity as a challenge to yourself, you might find your true gift and talent to share with the world. You might now work in an office in administration, enjoying the days with your colleagues, taking up a new challenge in floristry, and discovering this is where your joy is. Our joy brings us rewards. It can change your life.

When you are challenging yourself, you feel fulfilled and confident, and this will reflect in all your relationships, improving them or showing cracks in them. Either way, the ultimate part of the journey is to learn and grow, to share, and to be filled with joy.

When we are stimulated, we are in balance, and our health is in balance. When we are frustrated and agitated daily, this builds up. In effect, each day you continue to feel like this, you lay another brick on your wall. You become heavier, tired, achy, and generally feel like all you want to do is sit and watch the television when you get home. Now the biggest challenge is to jump over this wall or go on knock it down. Use all your strength to push it out of your way, coming through to learn and coming through to challenge and to live in joy! I'm right behind you.

be challenged. be active. be health. be joy. be love. be life. be happy. belifehappy.

Love: Senses and Spinning

. . . .

1 July 2010

In our lifetime, we will experience love from our relationships around us, friends, family, and partners. Some of us feel a love missing inside of us, and keep searching until we find it. Those with focus find their love was inside them all along. It wasn't hiding; it just needed a little help igniting.

Love: Senses

Love is beauty in the eyes. Love feels warm, soft, protective, and safe. Love is nurturing. Love the connection and aroma. Love the sound of their breathing.

What is being described above is any living thing – human, animal, plant – and the elements of the air, water, fire, and earth.

We all have our own beauty, our own protection to offer, and our own unique aroma and sound. (If we were to taste of anything, I'd most definitely be a victoria sponge, or maybe a carrot cake; actually I'd be a tea party!)

When we awaken in ourselves and feel our own love and bliss, we open our eyes to the beauty around us. We begin to be thankful and absorb the energy of the beauty around us. When we feel these feelings, they work through and around us. Life becomes love, and loving becomes living.

This is the transition we are approaching for those who want to. There is a huge emphasis on love and feelings, remembering that we have immense senses that we have in the past ignored with our busy life. Who would forget the smell of a baby? The unconditional love of your dog? The first words you heard your child say? Observe your world in full colour. What we have, had, or want becomes irrelevant, and the importance and communication shifts towards love and relationships with others. Share the gifts you have found or are finding and learn about the past to move on to the future.

Love is experienced in all aspects of our life. We cannot ignore it, and we each perceive it differently. Love is an individual emotion, and there is a stream of people across the globe joining together to share the high vibrations of love through their words, thoughts and actions. We each benefit from this stream of love as we give and receive love each day.

Immerse yourself in you, with time for you to connect to your source. Your love. Through meditation (walking, jogging, yoga, tai chi, cycling – anything that stills your mind), you can focus your intention on love.

Exercise

Love: Spinning

Sit in a chair, placing your feet firmly on the ground. Relax your shoulders, and rest both your hands on your knees. Relax your shoulders. Now plant your feet into the ground. Feel the earth around your feet. Feel safe and grounded.

Close your eyes; for a few minutes, focus inside your body and go towards your heart. What do you see? What do you hear? What do you feel? For these few moments, become your body and heart. Pay attention to what you feel. Do you feel yourself smiling, or do you feel sick?

Now keeping your focus on your heart, imagine it has become a beautiful radiant white light with pink rays. The light moves clockwise from your heart. Are your moving the light clockwise? Keep focusing and feel the light start to spin. How do you feel now?

Now take your attention back into your head, wriggle your toes through the earth, and take three deep breaths as you open your eyes and bring your attention back into the room.

This is a quick and simple exercise you can do as often as you wish to focus the intention of your day and your moments in your day and fill them with love.

Love yourself. Your mind and body. belifehappy. x.

Change from Within, Creates Change Without

....

5 July 2010

With no action, we create no change, and we stay the same. This is fact. Change is required only when we are unhappy with the present, past, or future, and by creating a happy outcome in the present, this will impact our future. The past is something we all deal with in our own way. We might box it up and store it in the garage to one day reopen it, or we open the boxes (when we are ready) and process past events and memories. Where there are painful memories, we learn and accept to release the pain and simply have memories.

For most in the busy world with work, families, and a social life to keep up with, we tend to live in the future of what has to be done and what if we did, and living in the past remembering when we were not so busy or blaming the past for what we have now.

Finding that present state now is something I've been getting back to. In 2008, I started meditation to help me through and gain strength whilst grieving, and while working, I lost track a little. By 2009, I was spending the whole year with regular reading, meditation, self-healing, and a full year of personal development. (This was my choice.) This year, distractions and fear have crept in. Then after a few weeks of feeling a little off, I got back into it and what a difference. My energy levels are back up! I've been reading, meditating for thirty minutes a day, watching wonderful movies, walking, doing new things, and meeting new people.

Do we realise how much change within changes us without?

It was only yesterday through a small chain of events which led me to meet a new person with whom I have a great deal in common on a coaching, change and fundraising level and stood next to a lady I hadn't seen for over three years. I would see this lady every morning in our local coffee shop for my morning cup of tea. (This was Emma who was a marketing manager.) Now in front of her, I commented, "I used to wear glasses," with which she replied, "Yes I knew there was something different about you, and whilst I watched you talking it's as though those glasses have come off and a whole new person is stood here!"

I wore glasses for fifteen years, and at the time I booked the laser surgery, I had committed to changing my life. I wonder now whether I hid behind those glasses, and I let the glasses determine who I was. I allowed my glasses to project me (and my excuses and limitations) and ultimately the without would be how I was perceived.

The glasses haven't changed me. The change within created the change without. This is the crux of all change. When change comes from without, it is not decided by us, and unless it agrees with our internal values and perceptions, it isn't going to work unless you make a change to accept, improve, or leave it. Change from within is hard work. (Those words just typed themselves!) It is hard work. As emotions are released and beliefs change, your outside world, the people in it, the work you do, and the things you enjoy doing (or thought you did!) all start to change.

This lady had known me maybe eighteen months, not seen me for three years, and saw a change from within in the space of five minutes. What did my friends and family see and feel? Well, that's the hard part and the joyous part. I have met new people and have new friends, and the friends in my life who were friends with me before accept and love me through my growth, as does my family. They see the positive change. The friends who leave us and we leave are part of the journey and of their journey. Look back with love.

Recognise change from within and work through it. The change is in response to your higher self guiding you to be who you are in your true light, with your true purpose. It is a life where you do not feel a battle, and a life where your talent, skill, knowledge, and kindness shine and radiate. We are unique with the purpose for each of us to share. Take a step forward today; create a space and time to be still; and allow yourself to feel calm, safe, and loved. You are.

I love sharing this journey with you.

Love: Home

· ·

8 July 2010

As you open the door into your home, you feel peace, comfort, security, and love. Where is home?

We arrive in the world inside our house. We begin to make this home as we learn and develop. Within our house, we might have a few maintenance issues: new guttering, subsidence, cracks in the walls. We might decide to decorate and have a new fresh look inside and out. Our house is important. It protects us.

Our house will show us signs as we settle in (are you settled in your house?) of things we need to look after:

- Do you have any cracks in the wall you papered over?
- Are you having trouble closing the shed door?
- Is the airing cupboard overflowing?
- Do you find it hard to keep on top of the tidying and cleaning?

Another thing with our house is that we invest in it. We commit to maintaining this structure to look after us. We pay others to fix it, or we learn how to fix it.

How does your house become your home?

- Are you living in it?
- Do you feel settled?

- Are you feeling a little anxious?
- Tired and drained?

Exercise

Go back now, and remember a time when your house felt like home. Describe to yourself what you can see. How did you feel, and what would it take you to create that feeling again?

Whilst we might believe we have a house, we cannot take our home for granted. "Don't run away from home as your problems will still be there." Have you heard that before? It's just like papering over the cracks. If you were to fix the crack and then redecorate, you would have faced the crack and taken a positive action to move forward.

- How bright is your home?
- Does it feel comfortable?
- Would you pass an energy inspection?
- What would happen when you pull back all your blinds and curtains, open all your windows, and flush your house with light and lots of air?
- Does your home feel relaxed and calm?

We enter this lifetime with a contract for the house we moved into. It is our responsibility to create a loving, kind, and peaceful home for us and to share with the other houses in the street. We do move house eventually. The home we create, however, stays with us, and we just modify, refresh, and make it more beautiful each time.

A home full of light is a home full of love.

Reconnect with the love inside your house and reconnect with your home.

be love. be life. be happy. belifehappy.

Lifetime Achievements

. . . .

12 July 2010

Journey of a Lifetime

The journey runs faster and faster as a goal approaches. We are seeing and feeling the results from the action we have committed to as part of a change and as part of a personal achievement. Success surrounds achievement, and whilst our efforts are not always rewarded the first time round, remember what you learned from the experience.

The next few months are about goal achievement for me. In eighty days I will be setting off to walk for six days on the Great Wall of China. Eight months ago, this thought had not entered my mind, so on the final day of the trek, I will be thinking about how each section and experience of my journey to this goal created the sense of achievement I imagine I will be feeling!

There are also life goals we have, and some people are lucky to achieve these through their own commitment and focus (so it's not luck that creates it.) These include climbing mountain peaks, sailing across the ocean, speaking a new language – anything we set ourselves as a lifetime achievement.

- What is your lifetime achievement?
- Have you achieved it?
- Are you working towards one?
- What are you doing to create the achievement?

Since I was a young girl, I loved to write and daydreamed of living in a beautiful wooden house in Canada (I've never been). The snow is all around, and the only way to go out to get groceries is to dig a path from the front door to the road and walk there, all wrapped up. I can still, right now, visualise that dream.

I am on a chair, wooden, looking out of a hatched window, painted white, on to the garden, and there is a very tall chestnut tree that stands above the house. I feel calm and at peace, and I have lots of A4 white paper around me. In front of me is my desk, and on it, in the middle, is a typewriter, and I am writing a novel. Now this daydream occurred when I was around twelve years old. (We didn't use computers, and what was a laptop?)

At school, I was told my English grades were not high enough for me to go to university to do English and that I'd not make it as a writer (creation of limiting belief.) Instead, I was directed down the line of creativity through design and communication and then through business and marketing. A side track. Then during my A levels, I wrote an English language piece, words from my heart. I got an A. My first A at English A level.

Several times, I have approached writing a book, and five years ago, I took some time out and started. Yes, I got sidetracked. I have three books started, and it wasn't until a couple of months ago that I started to think about what it was I wanted to achieve. The book came back into my head. The book is in my heart, and I'd lost touch with my heart for a few years. Now I am only guided by it. So now is the time for me to start working on my lifetime goal. The stepping stones and the sidetracks are all part of the lifetime achievement, as each one adds to the background story.

- What is your story?
- What words describe your world and describe today?

- When you close your eyes do you see, feel, and hear your lifetime achievement?

Not all of us know our lifetime achievement, and some of us will dismiss it, thinking it's ridiculous when you have so many responsibilities. We sometimes just require a little connection with our goal getter to put us back on the path of our conscious plans. And that's why, I guess, you are here reading this.

Give: Into Awareness

13 July 2010

The beauty abounds all your surroundings. Do you see it, do you feel it, and can you hear it? Embrace the reality of your world, and we can all do this by stopping for a few moments to notice the colour of the fields, the colour of the lawn, and the shape of the clouds. How does the outside breeze feel as it touches your skin?

What we see, feel, hear, and believe to be our reality is what we allow our awareness to be. By investing in those few moments of awareness of our world, we find a greater peace from the stillness and a greater love for our world. When there is a feeling of respect and admiration of our world, we find this reflection in the mirror.

Give your awareness to your world today. See the beauty, feel the air, hear the stillness, and feel love.

Your Love

How bright is the sun, the moon, and the stars,
They are only as bright as the eyes that are,

Aware of their light and of their love,
Are you aware of the world above?

Above and below, within and without,
Do you feel happiness, or do you feel doubt?

Feel the radiance of your light,
Feel the radiance of your love,

Above and beyond,
Up flying high and bright,
Share now, and become aware of this beautiful sight.

Written by Emma Lannigan

Love: You Are Allowed To

. . . .

15 July 2010

We are allowed to love ourselves.

We grow up with individual perceptions of love: what it is, how it feels, and how it works. Are we told about how to love ourselves? We hear as we grow up how love hurts, love is painful, love is something we get over, or that love is simply lust and not to be interfered with. Depending on our generation, this will have a great effect on how we perceive love in general. However, love is mostly described quite negatively, so it isn't any wonder when I ask people if they love themselves and they respond with a look of confusion and say they really had not thought about it.

Have you thought about whether you are in love with yourself? Is this another silly notion of this early part of the millennium? Or can you begin to feel, as you look around, and understand that whatever generation you are in, there is a definitive shift occurring where love comes from within and then lights up our world.

Whether you are able to grasp this new concept of love, isn't it beautiful that this option breeds positive messages about love? Would that breed more successful loving relationships with partners, family, and friends?

When we have woken up in the morning and the skies appear grey, the journey to work a drag, and the rain another irritation, could all these things be just how we see them to be: an irritation? And what would happen if we chose to wake up and embrace the grey skies for their energy and passion, to enjoy the calmness of our journey to work, and to feel the rain refresh the nature around us? Can we agree this change of mindset is possible?

You're not allowed ... a statement we will have heard at some stage of our life. What it was that we were not allowed is likely to affect what we allow for ourselves. If we work in an environment where laughter is stifled (work is for working, not for enjoying), you're not likely going to feel any love inside, particularly for that job. Where you are in a situation, whether at work or at home, the level of love within that environment will affect the level of love you associate with.

Within is a reflection of without: change within and change without.

There's no need to panic, though, because there is enough love for every one of us. And we are all allowed to connect to this unlimited source.

It costs nothing, and it brings peace and joyfulness back into our life, as well as confidence and self-esteem, and once we have learned that we can use it all the time and it is okay, this love flows through and around everyone and everything in our life.

Ten ways to tell when you are connected to your love within:

1) Look in the mirror. What is the first word, thought, or action you have?
2) Sit quietly close your eyes. What do you feel?
3) Say no to a friend or family member because you have something you would like to do for you (and your family). How do you feel?

4) Drive, walk, or bike into the country or nature park. Notice what you can see now. Does it look brighter? Can you hear sounds you hadn't noticed before?

5) When you walk, how does that feel? Straighter, taller, more relaxed?

6) Stop and ask before you leave the house in the morning for one thing you would like to happen today. Before you go to bed, look and think through the day's events and ask whether it happened?

7) The house looks like tornado has been through it, and you notice a broken vase. What is your reaction?

8) Time manages itself, and you feel like you are in control of it. Are you feeling rushed?

9) Going on holiday is no longer the most stressful event (along with house moves and divorce) and becomes an enjoyable experience.

10) You sleep to rest, and you sleep well, knowing and feeling always that you are love, you are loved, and you are safe and protected.

All our responses and reactions when we feel love within are calm, kind, and respectful of others. This new love is one to embrace and share; it offers acts of kindness and supports us all on our journey, providing more ease, less disease, more love, and less fighting. We are moving to bring in the balance we all lost.

We have already found our love and experienced glimpses through our own desire for happiness today, tomorrow, and every day. We can practice to connect to our love from within, and the more we connect, the more we see it reflected in our daily actions, words, and choices. Love: We are allowed to see it, feel it, hear it, and, most importantly, share it.

be love. be life. be happy. belifehappy.

Sharing New Horizons

. . . .

19 July 2010

Perception plays a leading role in personal development. Having worked in a highly motivational environment where self-help bibles were referred to on many occasions, my perception was that self-help was therapy, I didn't need therapy, and a Bible wasn't going to work for me either. Our attitudes and beliefs direct us and can also limit us. I'd grown up with many Bibles around the house; however, I had not felt inclined to read one.

A few more years on, I found my own personal development. And with my perception of the words *personal development*, I can actually visualise me developing and moving forward.

It takes only ourselves to travel and choose to travel, remembering there is no destination, just stops on the way with the idea to accept, learn, let go of what you see in the rear-view mirror, and then keep on driving forward.

2010 has been a slowly progressive year, calmer in pace than 2009, although on paper, I have still been developing in a settled way. When I reviewed my goals in June of this year, I spent a few days thinking about them, wrote them in a notebook, and will leave them there until the end of the year. I am trusting that each day and moment, I am working towards these goals. One of them is my personal development. I am so happy and fulfilled when I am learning through books and people, and this year, I have been focusing on "doing" in areas of my life and not developing and realised what I was missing.

Time, creating, managing, and allowing time to do, be, and have what we want in our lives requires balance. I've started to review my own balance, and it's creating amazing opportunities.

Review, recharge, regrowth. A cycle.

Give: Randomly

. . . .

20 July 2010

At some point, I am sure you will have come across the term *random acts of kindness*. This type of kindness in action is not planned, has no expectations, and is done purely from the heart to help another.

You might have experienced one of these actions and not even realised it had a name, and the same for those of you who have simply helped another and again not named it. Last week, I received three random acts of kindness. These were from three individuals on different days.

The first involved a car park pay machine. You know those days when you have an errand to run and have everything focused on the errand and forgot the change for the parking meter? Already there, I went up to a man who was stood there and asked if he had any change. With no shops nearby, I hoped he would help me and he did. I had only a little change, and with that, he said he'd give to me the €1 I needed to pay. I thanked him.

A few days later, I was at the supermarket, and I went to have my fruit and vegetables weighed. The member of staff didn't know the price, and I didn't either, so he went off to get one. In the meantime, a lady was waiting behind me so another member of staff took my item, weighed it, put in a price, and threw it at me so he could serve the next lady. The first member of staff came running back and started to argue with the man, which resulted in my fruit being snatched back and reweighed with the correct price. I thanked the first man as he did not have to do what he did, and he did it because he knew it was right. His kindness saved me money on my groceries. The second man's actions spoke for him.

I'm now going to add that both the above experiences occurred with a language barrier, so these conversations and exchanges all happened without direct words. How is your body language today?

The third act of kindness was a lady who sent me a text message to wish me well on my charity trek and a charity event I have arranged locally to fundraise for the Mental Health Foundation. I had received a bit of coverage in the weekly national paper in my local section, and it has my number on. This lady took the time to send me a message sharing an experience she had had and to personally pass on her support. I replied with thanks for this lady's time and kindness. Is there someone you would like to send your support to and haven't got around to it?

Create the time as your actions, words, and feelings are to be shared and to support others.

This year, I have also learned a lot about other random kindness, where people I have met and become friends with have gone on to introduce me to other people, who have also become friends. Money cannot buy the random act of kindness, it comes through sharing knowledge and experiences. You have so many gifts and talents to share. Believe in yourself and watch and feel how your random kindness starts to create changes in your life and in the lives of others.

To receive kindness, we often need to look within ourselves and review how kind are we and how we respond to kindness. Again, this response isn't just in our words. It is in how we look, our facial expressions, how we stand, our posture, and the tone we use in our words. You can consciously be kind today. When you start your day, remind yourself to be kind. Without your knowing, your kindness will radiate, and as you help others, they too will help you. Like attracts like. Kindness attracts kindness.

be kind. believe. be life. be happy. belifehappy.

Play: Time

● ●

21 July 2010

Has anyone else noticed we're approaching the summer? Schools will soon be out for the summer break in the UK, and it will be time for more work/life balance, juggling to give to families, to find time to play, to find time to feel and explore our love, and to learn from each moment. The summer is a time of beautiful weather and comes with it the high expectation that this is a time to relax and enjoy. However, more and more of us find the joy has been lost somewhere between work and home.

The simplicity of a day also seems to be lost when people spend most of the day reminding themselves of 'how much they have to do and so little time,' and with this creates so much to do and not enough time!

The biggest challenge for us all is to embrace our own time. There are countless books available and training courses to teach us to find our own time, perhaps the most well-known is *The Power of Now* by Erkhart Tolle. Isn't the other big challenge finding the time to read these?

The point here is that the fact there are books and courses to teach us how to manage, create, and own our time indicates that it is possible. What we have to decide is whether it is really what we want (to be in control of our time)? When you have reached the point where you know and practice everyday control and ownership of your time, you will be able to be, do, and have anything. Wow!

All from time. Time is endless.

So my greatest tip for the summer is to enjoy each day. Have an outline plan and list of places and activities you can do. Involve everyone, aim to have a balance of everyone's expectations, and achieve them. This way, time will only be spent where it is required, and therefore, there will be enough created for everyone to enjoy themselves.

We spend time, and we invest time, so maybe one further tip is to spend and invest as you would with your money. Do so wisely to cover basic needs, to have enjoyment, and to have treats. The great thing is there is so much to do out there that doesn't cost money, but maybe costs a little from your creativity bank and is so much more fun!

Let's go!

Love: Your Reflection

. . . .

22 July 2010

Exercise

This is a gentle meditation to guide you and reconnect within, in mind, body, and spirit.

Find somewhere peaceful with no interruptions or a telephone. Create a comfortable space and room temperature.

Read this through now, or ask a friend or partner to read it to you.

Sit comfortable on a chair, with your back straight and your shoulders relaxed. Close your eyes and feel your feet plant themselves into the ground. Feeling secure and protected, turn your attention to your breathing. As you inhale, see and feel the air move through your body, cleansing all the way down into your stomach. As you exhale, feel the air leave your body, exhaling it all out. Now take two more deep breathes. Filling your body with light and exhaling your day, relaxing your mind and relaxing your body.

Notice how you have entered a beautiful wooden lodge in a natural parkland. You can feel the lodge breathing with you. In front of you is a small oak staircase that leads to the gardens and the lake. The staircase has a beautiful rich green carpet, and to your left is a handrail to help you feel secure and safe as you start to climb down the stairs. Count as you take your first step, ten, then nine, eight.

You start to feel the green carpet softening and your body feels heavier as it relaxes. Seven, six, breathing slowly with each step. Five, four, three, the light from outside is brighter as you get closer to the window. Two, one.

After the last step, walk through the lobby, observing the richness of the oak, and walk towards the doors leading to the gardens. Follow the stone pathway lined with a bright array of flowers, which you can smell each scent as the light breeze passes your face.

Ahead you see the lake. The richest blue water, sparkling through the trees lining the lake. As you walk through the entrance, the glistening light from the water catches your eye. The light sparkles from the water surrounding you, dancing like butterflies.

There is a wide sturdy wooden bridge in the middle of the lake, and you begin to walk across it, noticing when you look down that you can see your reflection. Stop when you get to the middle and look into the water. What do you see? Look and absorb the beauty of your reflection. Youthfulness, health, and vitality abounds. Feel the healing energy from the lake. The lake reflecting your beauty, your kindness, your light, and your love.

As you look at your reflection, affirm to yourself I am confident, I am health, I am kindness, I am happiness and joy, I am peace, I am love, and I am loved. You can add more now as you spend a few minutes noticing what you feel and where you feel those feelings from your reflection. What can you hear, and what do you see? Let all your negative feelings float away, and send your positive feelings into your reflection in the lake. Embrace the peace and safety of the lake and enjoy you.

What have you learned? Now start to walk back to the edge of the lake, observing as you take the last few steps off the wooden bridge the beauty this tranquil place has given you.

Take a deep breath in, and exhale as you now start to walk back to the lodge. Go back through the doors and to the small oak wooden staircase, and as you walk up to the top count with me from one to ten. One, two, three, become aware of your breathing. Four, five, become aware of your body. Six, wriggle your toes and fingers. Seven, eight, become aware of the chair and the room. Nine, open your eyes. Ten, take a few deep breathes and drink a glass of water.

It is important to remember our inner beauty and light. We always have it, today, tomorrow, and every day.

We share our light and often forget to turn it up for ourselves. Be your shining light and be love. be life. be happy.

Back to School

· ·

6 September 2010

I've sat here for a moment and looked back through my time capsule mind to see and seek a memory of my first day back at school. The first thing is the smell of my new leather shoes and my school bag. I can see the brilliant whiteness of my shirt and see my neatly ruffled socks (there was an art to it!). That's it. There are no longer any feelings attached to that day. University. I remember my first day. I can recall the feelings and conversations like a movie playing in front of me now.

At back-to-school time, whether you are a parent or not, we all feel the new start approaching, the autumn clothes, the darker nights, and the slow bubble of excitement of festivities drawing closer.

What was summer for? What did we do? What did we learn? While many of you reading this now will have maybe taken a week or two to take a family break, how do you feel now? Have you still got the feeling of summer? What is your summer feeling?

It is so easy to fall back into a routine in the working week, and now with the schools back, the traffic on the roads in the morning will be busier. More traffic, more (what are you thinking?), more stress. Or more time to sing to your favourite songs on the radio?

This is a great time to step up a gear with any goals you have or dreams you would like to turn into goals. Time is always on your side. It's just waiting for you to make the decision about what you want to be and do.

At the beginning of the year, you start off with fresh ideas and positive dreams, and by the end of January, gloom has left half of you thinking that it won't happen this year. It still can. This is your new start Monday. School's back: What do you want to learn?

You can achieve anything. That sounds rather grand: anything! We learn each day. Over a period of time, we build up the resources and skills required to fulfil a goal (exams and career or life.) With our goals now, we can create them and start to work towards them every day. In your heart, you know what it is you want to achieve and with this knowledge you are more likely to be successful.

Going back to the classroom, after the key subjects, when choosing your pathway subjects for GCSE or A level, did you choose from the heart?

With your career path, did you plan it? If so, did it come from within and with passion?

Success and joy in our work comes from within. It is as difficult as choosing those subjects; however, changing jobs, training for promotion, and changing careers can be life-changing.

School teaches us how to learn. We grow each day through creativity; laughter; giving to others; sharing knowledge; playing and having fun; and loving friendships, relationships, and ourselves.

today. tomorrow. everyday. give. play. love. learn.

Let's fly. Let's go!

Give: Fears and Phobias
to the Past

. . . .

7 September 2010

The greatest gift we can give our children and young friends is the gift of our wisdom. This is to give them freedom of knowledge to explore, create, and imagine their world.

What would happen if we taught our children our fears and phobias? We would be creating more of the same of what we already have. Limitations. And does it matter that our children sense our fear and therefore create their own fear? What about the fears our children develop on their own?

Fears and phobias can have lasting effects on our physical and emotional well-being. Each time we are confronted with a fear or phobia, our bodies react through hormone responses known as fight or flight. This reaction causes stress on our body systems, and to continuously do this creates a build-up and results in long-term health effects.

With each situation we ignore or avoid facing, we build up more of a wall. For free-flowing health and well-being, the aim is to have no walls.

So it's easy to identify this with ourselves as adults. What about children?

An example with a heart-glowing ending comes from a little boy aged five and a half. He had swimming lessons, and his daddy is a very strong swimmer. He is not afraid of water, only of swimming in the sea. While on holiday one day, the family were going to the beach, which to him meant no swimming pool. He was a little upset; however, the thought of building sandcastles soon made up for it. Down at the beach, his daddy and mummy were going in the sea, and he wanted to, but he kept pulling away from the water. At this point, there was a choice: to comfort this little man with his fear of swimming in the sea and take him back to the swimming pool or make it fun and help him conquer his fear.

For the whole afternoon, he jumped all the waves, being carried out with his daddy to experience the bigger waves and swimming with his mummy by the shore. The following trip to the beach, this little boy went in the sea with both parents, and by the afternoon, he would run in with his daddy. You would not have ever known he had a fear of the sea.

With a memory from a previous holiday and from going in the sea, he had created a link to this memory/event and the sea. The sea had not created the fear directly; however, in his mind, it was the trigger. After asking him to explain the reason, supporting the reason, and showing him how to overcome this fear, next holiday, his memories will be of how he conquered the sea last summer!

For us adults, it's not as simple to conquer a fear in a day or two. We often don't have someone to hold our hand, and we also have more than one event to trigger the fear. In fact, we are more likely to have a whole card system of event after event. Therefore, we have many excuses not to do something because of the fear.

Fears of driving, heights, and going out in busy crowded places (to start with) can lead to a very limiting lifestyle. It often creeps up on us over a period of time, and by the time we recognise it, the fear has not just limited us, but it has also created disease.

Just as we can help our children overcome their fears and phobias so they can enjoy a free-flowing freedom in the early learning years, we can also experience free-flowing freedom and overcome our limiting fears. Your life can be free and help you and others around you live with your fears.

Give the gift of your free-flowing inner world to those around you. Share your light and shine brightly.

be giving. be free. be love. be life. be happy.

Focus Pocus

. . . .

13 September 2010

With a clear goal, determination, and commitment, you will achieve success! Focus pocus! It's like magic. Go set your intentions, and get moving!

In nineteen days, I will be off doing something I honestly could have not even conceived ten months ago. In fact, ten months ago, I had only just moved country (again!).

I've spent the weekend preparing my packing and paperwork for my first charity trek, and during this time, I started to reflect on what I was about to achieve. After nearly eight months of training and fundraising, I am about to actually complete the challenge. I know in my heart that each day when I was training, if there was an inch of "I can't do this today," I'd remember why it was important to do it and why I was doing it. It's important to train to reduce injuries for when I complete the actual walk, and the money I have raised for this walk will support a charity that researches mental illness, the Mental Health Foundation (the big goal.)

There has been quite a recurrent theme when I am asked about my personal drive to complete things. I look at what I want to achieve and then look at the stepping stones to achieve the goal. To be physically able to do this walk, I have needed to commit to training. What would happen if I didn't? I would let myself down, as well as the charity I am supporting and the friends and family who are supporting me to achieve my goal!

There are still ten months of reflection, and I'm also now able to see other things I have done that have contributed to where I am now. The full picture is not achieved; however, I'd say pretty much seventy-five percent of it is. This is of the vision board I created in December 2009. It's folded away, and I haven't looked at it; the other evening, a mental picture of the board came into view as if to remind me I am receiving what I wanted. I'd placed on it a charity trek and to be physically fit. Now there are some other things, too. However, I'm going to hold fire on those for now as we still have a few months before the end of the year.

The vision board helped me create a picture of what I wanted in my life this year, and without looking at it every day or fixating on it, I have worked towards achieving these things. In my true self, these are things that I do and can have.

Believing is crucial. Many times in the last ten months, I have often said to myself, *Maybe I should be normal and get a proper job.* I'm not sure of your perception; however, when I look back at those words, I know there is no *should* or *normal* or *proper*! They are simply perceptions. So I gamble with my life path and trust and believe that where it takes me is where I will go. Where I go is where I asked to go!

When the journey is not enjoyable, then it is time to change it. Changes often happen to keep us on the right path, and by embracing the changes and trusting and feeling they are right for your life path, you can follow and flow!

I look and see the changes that have happened within me over the last ten months. I've shown myself what I am capable of and learned to believe in myself. I have become more aware of myself and of others and listened to how I feel and had the confidence to make decisions which in fear I would not have done. I feel happy, I feel joy, and I feel love.

We all have the ability to change or start working towards a goal that ignites these real emotions. Life is amazing. You are amazing. (ZING!)

Start this week by reviewing what you have achieved this year. Is there anything you still would like to do before Christmas? Write down your achievements, what you have learned, and what you would like to do. Through words and images (your photographs, for example), you will see how much you have grown and where you would like to go next.

Life is a journey. You can sit on the sofa and watch another world, or you can get up, put your coat on, and create your own!

Let's go! Review, focus, and achieve!

The Sky is Grey, and it's Monday Morning. What Next?

20 September 2010

Last Friday, I held a small coffee morning as part of my fundraising for the Mental Health Foundation. During the event, I enjoyed several discussions about how I got into this.

You see, having experienced depression to the degree where I no longer saw my reflection in a mirror ten years ago, I do understand the journey out of the dark tunnel. I also understand about choices – tough life choices, including what to eat because I had no money (many students experience this) and switching off medication and a ventilator (I wasn't on my own for that decision; however, it was extremely difficult to agree).

I therefore do often discuss with others about the future for someone who has experienced a form of mental illness such as depression. I personally believe it does not go away. and in fact, the illness is actually an awakening sign for the person to make changes in their life. It represents a cross-section where we are required to regain contact with our inner self and listen and feel the best course of action. It is a huge learning experience. Once experienced and the person's awareness is increased, these crossroads appear more and more. It is ever the opportunity to grow to experience a newness of life. And this comes out in the light after the darkness of depression.

I don't know if there will be any of you reading this thinking;

- I can relate to this, and I've not experienced depression.
- How does this motivate me today?

At some point in our lives, we are presented with lessons to learn, and we approach these through free will and the choice to accept them, ignore them, or move on. Either way, it is always our choice.

Choice is your motivation. As I sat with several people and discussed choice, more so than ever, it was crystal clear. The only answer to anything is choice. Your own personal choice. Your responsibility. All within you.

Can you feel the motivation? What is your motivation for today?

Write your answer here:

Look at the words. Are they negative? If so, what would happen if you changed your motivation today into a positive? What would happen if each morning, you created a positive motivation? Would it be worth it?

Happiness and ultimate joy is a choice. It doesn't appear like magic. It feels like magic. However, we can work towards achieving this every day, and if we do, we are rewarded with the greatest emotion: love.

Your motivation for today creates each moment of happiness, and each moment of happiness creates a period of happiness. Just imagine all those periods of happiness becoming a lifetime of happiness.

Be life happy. Make a choice.

No one else can create your happiness.

give. play. love. learn how to create it yourself today, tomorrow, and every day.

Give: Shocking Life into Perspective

. . . .

21 September 2010

Awareness is something we think we are aware of. Right now, you'll be aware of the day, what clothes you are wearing, what the weather is like, and maybe the morning news. What else are you aware of? And what do the things you are aware of make you feel like? How many of the things you are aware of right now are sending positive feelings?

It's no wonder how our awareness becomes limited with the amount of noise we have, and in terms of noise, I refer to the numerous messages we receive each day via the radio, television news programmes, commercials, newsletters, memos, text messages, Facebook, Twitter, blogs, and face-to-face conversations.

Giving is very much about awareness. It's an action where we give any of these things to help another, through kindness, knowledge, support, caring, listening. Again, the list is endless like the list of noise.

Through the noise is a big haze of daily routine with clouds of negative smog floating around. This is the time to give ourselves a shock and let the sun shine and flood our world with light. Then we can put life into perspective.

It's not to be underestimated: Our decisions, choices, and actions are based on our current perspective, but are you seeing what is really there? You can't see the woods for the trees: This is a great reference to help others; however, when we are searching for the woods, we really are blinded. The noise creates the haze and reduces our line of vision to our goals.

Once we give ourselves the time and respect we deserve to give ourselves, the haze begins to lift, the beautiful green trees appear with their fresh smell, and we feel alive.

Now we can give to others. Calming down the noise is key when you are on or feeling overwhelmed. Ways to reduce noise can be as simple as finding a few minutes a day just to be still and quiet, to turning off the radio for a few hours, reducing the time you watch TV, or swapping your gossip magazines for a literary escape into a book you've had on the shelf for ages.

When you balance giving in your life, you will easily give to others and always have abundance in all areas of your life. It is not about sacrificing what you have; your giving is always returned. However, watch your expectations: Giving comes with no expectations in return. Give because you want to and because you can. Today, you will make a difference.

Turn down the noise each day and give peace to yourself to be able to offer your kindness to others.

be giving. be you. be love. be light. be life. be happy.

Love: Sensory Awareness

· ·

23 September 2010

We've talked about awareness more in line with vision, our actions and others' actions, creating our perspective on life now. How we feel emotionally and physically creates much more of our awareness like a sensory gift we often ignore or forget to consult with.

How we feel emotionally is becoming the new way to live, like it or not. It's happening whether you're in or not. The programmes you watch, the books flooding the bookshelves, and the language used in commercials: We are all moving towards a new era where our emotions and feelings will lead the way. For some, this is true now.

So what's changed? Have we become bored of materialism? Is the fifty-plus-inch TV just not cutting it anymore? Feelings of emotional and physical come through to one simple stream of energy. Energy vibrates at different ranges from low (material) to high (spiritual) frequency. Our world has become dense with low-frequency energy, and an imbalance has occurred. Naturally, as through history, changes occur, and whilst we might not see it now, what we are all doing is moving towards creating a balance. To do this, we are letting go, emotionally and physically.

Ouch, the drain! From carrying our emotional history around in our physical bodies to releasing it, we are embarking on a lighter life! (Doesn't that sound amazing?!) To get to the lighter light, we have to embrace the emotional history and let it go. This is not an easy journey. If it were, we would have all done this decades ago, and this imbalance wouldn't be occurring. Everything happens for a reason, and this is happening to teach us about the simplicity of life: what we have to be grateful for and how to love unconditionally.

Physically, we've been isolated into a world with commercialism that requires us to work like a hamster running on its wheel that sometimes forgets to step off for a break. We're exhausted and have no time to live, enjoy the gift of our senses, and be aware of the beauty that is within and around us in every moment.

Instead, many have cut this connection and see only the harsh reality of life, such as bills, mortgage, rent, petrol, food prices, clothing, etc. This is a reality. However, you have a gift to balance your awareness with feeling the greatness of who you are, where you are, and the people who are with you now.

It's time to break down the walls and smile at a stranger.

Our sense of touch is immense. Look at your arms, find a hair, and hover your finger above it. Can you feel it? Just one finger over one hair, and that is your entire awareness. Your smile sends signals through your body, so that when others see your smile, they feel it through your energy.

When you think of something upsetting, perhaps a conversation or event, where do you feel that in your body? How does it make you feel? Now think about something that makes you feel happy. Again, where do you feel that? How does it make you feel?

This is awareness. We're just learning how to uses these sense to their full potential, and to make it part of every day, we just have to practice. Be aware.

With increased sensory awareness, you raise your vibration and create balance within yourself. It is a balance you can share with others. Feeling joy is a gift. Accept and live it.

be balance. be love. be life. be happy. belifehappy.

Motivation

. . . .

27 September 2010

Motivation is a huge part of my life, more so this week ahead, ready for next Saturday. I am always feeling a drive to do the things I want to achieve, and this for me highlights all the things I've not really wanted to do. Ten months ago, I was walking along Riccos Beach in Paphos listening to Frank Sinatra on my iPod. It was my birthday. With the wintry skies and breeze, I set off, and my mind began to drift to what I could do to challenge my walking. Where would these hour-long walks on the same path take me?

It was time to change and find longer, more challenging routes. I'd not previously been a religious fitness person (judgment), just simply balanced and healthy. Fitness was my walking and occasional swimming (nothing excessive!) On this day, however, I knew it was time to do something. When I got home, I got out my vision board and saw I had put on a picture of a charity trek. I then asked myself whether I could really do such a thing. After a little research, I had booked myself on a trip four weeks later with a fitness training plan and a fundraising target. Again, I asked whether I could I really do this?

We say we want to do something and talk about it, and it can be months or years later when we think back and remind ourselves of the thing we haven't done. The best form of motivation I have found is regret. For everything I think about doing, being, or having, I appear to have a personal process that, without me consciously knowing, looks and assesses whether I will have any regret if I don't do it.

All my major goals are achieved because there would be regret if they were ignored. They all challenge me and help me grow. Thankfully, we're not all the same, and our individual motivational strategies differ. On one hand, this is a blessing, and on the other, it allows us to understand that we are not all motivated or driven to achieve the same things. We become aware and respect other people's dreams.

We each know in our hearts what we want from our lifetime, and whilst we might have lots of things in common with our friends and colleagues, we might not be driven by the same things. To a degree, we all seek encouragement to pursue and achieve our goals, and what we forget is that our friends will not always give us that encouragement because it is not necessarily important or worthwhile in their eyes.

Many people divert to completely stopping in their tracks of achieving a goal because they are not able to get the support they believe they should be getting.

You will only do, be, and have what you truly desire. Trying will lead to chasing until you become tired and give up. When you truly want to achieve something, you will do it on your own. You will always have support from yourself. A belief in yourself is enough to achieve anything you wish to achieve.

You, your friends, your family, and your colleagues all have their own motivations. Learn from others, and respect each others' dreams. And if your friends don't achieve their dreams, maybe it's because it wasn't theirs.

Ask yourself whether you have any regrets. Is there something you keep talking about and are not getting around to? Think about how you would feel if you did not achieve these things and then you will know where your motivation is (if any). You'll then know how to start taking steps forward and committing to your life experiences.

This journey is our own, and we meet people and share parts of our lives with people. However, ultimately, the experience is joy for everyone. When you follow your dreams, your dreams will follow you.

Be your dream.

Give: Thoughts of Kindness

· ·

28 September 2010

The simple action of thoughtfulness creates a simple act of kindness, and through this kindness, joy for someone else or something is created.

If we neglect a plant in our house or garden, it will become unhappy and wilt.

A simple thought has the power to change neglect to care and being thoughtful, benefiting your life, your environment, and the people who share it.

A grand gesture is great for that one moment it is received; however, they are seldom offered. Lots of small, kind thoughts and actions can create lots of moments of joy.

Giving is simple. Watch your world come alive with the brightness of your kindness today, tomorrow, and every day.

Love: Breathing for Clarity

· ·

30 September 2010

Today is a gift. You are the gift, and with a gift, we feel joy and happiness. Experience your gift with each breath you take, inhaling life into every cell in your body and exhaling everything we can let go of today.

We all have a blind spot, a point at which we cannot see what is there. Do we have a point at which we can no longer feel clarity?

At the point of stress, our body feels the stress from our mind, and the mixture collides to a point we can no longer feel or see a clear solution. Here, we have found our internal blind spot.

We each have a gift when we are born that unconsciously works, without reminder, to give us life. Breathing.

We can use our breathing to create clarity. Become aware of your breathing and allow it to show you clarity of the feeling and vision of what is in front of you to appear. The focus of inhaling allows us to focus on the goodness that is entering our body to provide fuel to each cell, flushing your arteries with light. As you exhale, allow your body to release all that it cannot use and does not want. Let it go.

As we breathe, our chest or stomach will raise and lower. Breathing from the chest is often referred to as shallow breathing; we do this in activity or stressful situations. Optimum breathing, used by sports professionals and people in relaxation, mediation, and yoga, for example, draws each breath by focusing on filling the space behind the belly button. Imagine a dark space being filled with light. As you inhale, fill the space with more energy, feeling bigger and stronger, and release on each exhalation all negativity you feel. There is no limit to the amount of confidence, health, calm, peace, happiness, joy, and love you can inhale.

We can use breathing to help us each day in all situations. Replace a few deep intentional breaths instead of negative harsh words that only add to your present state of blindness.

Allow your breathing to give you the vision of calm to make the right choices for you. Become aware of your breathing and think about what you are breathing in.

Enjoy your gift and its flow.

be life. be happy.

Are You Living Your Dream?

. . . .

1 October 2010

Five years ago, I arrived at Paphos International Airport. I'd already met some friends whilst I was there for three months on a trial run before committing to the move. So there I was, twenty-eight years old with a suitcase, a one-bedroom apartment, and a job interview. My dream was to enjoy life, without the stress and pressure from my previous career in marketing. So far, so good.

After one interview, I found an advert for another position with a much lower salary. However, it offered a little more security as I settled into my new life. By 19 September 2005, I had a job, an unpacked suitcase, and a one-bedroom apartment.

So far, so good. As my job progressed and I settled into this new life, I brought back my old one. Whether it was a sense of fear or a sense of security, I don't know. However, let's say it was not long before really my life in Cyprus was no different from my life in the UK. Work nine to five (although it felt a lot longer), Monday to Friday. Where was my dream life now?

Well, it was still here. "Wouldn't you rather have your career here in paradise?" I was asked. Well, I suppose it was paradise, for now.

The skies are blue, the sea beautiful, and the air refreshing. That's what I was writing, but I wasn't seeing, feeling, or hearing it. I felt air con in my home, air con in the elevator, air con in the car, air con in the office, and at five in the afternoon, we reverse that! Does this sound familiar?

I mainly work from home now and have the fortunate opportunity to get about and meet new people, and I love to ask why expats move to Cyprus and how they feel about it. What strikes me most is the lack of balance and happiness people have found but now feel stuck here. Where did their dreams go? One gentleman mentioned that on his drive to work years ago, he loved to look at the sunrise. Now, he couldn't remember the last time he noticed it or had the time to.

So where is the balance of living on the island of love with its glorious sun, sand, and mountain views?

I found third time lucky. The balance was within each of us. Only I could make the most of each day and the place I set out to call home. The vision for our dream can change. It's good for it to change and challenge us. However, the feeling we have about the vision is something we have control to change. We can shape the vision of our dreams and live them now!

Sometimes, we don't see or know what we have achieved because we are so busy. Start writing a list of what you have achieved this year for yourself, at work, and as a family.

Create Your Cake and Eat It!

· ·

5 October 2010

There are no coincidences and life is not ordinary.

In our minds, we consciously set goals for ourselves. How we achieve them comes down to how we work with our unconscious minds. The "Oh it's a silly idea" is perhaps an idea your unconscious mind was giving you to achieve a goal you set with your conscious mind. Why do you let your conscious mind put up blockers? For many reasons, and it is more often out of fear: fear of change.

Life is full of coincidences that we create to enjoy and experience as part of an extra-unordinary life.

My favourite way to relax is with a lovely cup of tea (preferably from a pot) and a slice of freshly baked cake. This might not be extraordinary from the outside; however, we can all create what we feel inside. Have your cake and eat it?: Have you ever thought about what it actually is implying?

Let's think about the cake. What type of cake is it? What is it made of? How is it made? The answers to these questions all create different taste experiences.

When you've decided on your cake and ingredients, you go to the supermarket and select the ingredients you want. Back at home with your mixing bowl, you start to mix up the ingredients, step by step, before placing the batter in your preheated oven. Now you wait for your delicious cake.

The process of defining our goals is similar to baking a cake:

- Identify a recipe (the taste, shape, and finishing – identify your goal)
- Select the type of ingredients (what resources do you require and want to add in)
- Timing and preparation (be specific, measurable, achievable, realistic, and timed)
- Enjoyment (if there is no joy, why would you be doing it?)
- Creating (doing anything that is new and different)
- Flexibility (adapting to changes and learnings along the way)
- Action (the cake doesn't bake on its own – your goal is not achieved without your input and action)
- Expectations (what is your desired result, what does it look like and feel like, and how big are those feelings?)
- Result (how will you know when you have achieved your goal, and what does your buzzer on the cooker sound like?)
- Achievement (whether it is the taste of your cake or of the feeling of your sense of achievement, remember the feeling, hold it in your mind and know you can experience that same feeling anytime you call upon it)

With your goals, you have a choice at each stage of the process to amend your course of action to achieve your desired outcome.

Failure comes only from nonaction.

When you have baked your cake, and it's not as you expected on the outside or on the inside, this is not a failure. From this you have the opportunity to learn how to improve when you make your next one!

Cakes (goals or priorities) are not just for big celebrations.

Goals and priorities are small and big and can be of equal importance. The small ones are just as important as the big ones as they take you a step closer to achieving your ultimate goal or dream.

Create and bake your cake so it brings you joy you can share with others.

"Everyone who Walks the Great Wall of China is a Hero" [Sasha, our guide]

· ·

11 October 2010

10:10 am on 10/10/2010, and I was checking in at Beijing Airport, the challenge complete, and now the journey home.

I'm sat at the departure gate thinking of you all and what and how I would write to describe the past nine days, which have felt like a lifetime in accomplishment and achievements.

With an open mind, I have been surprised, physically challenged far beyond my expectations, and culturally awakened to a different way of living. I also met and shared this experience with ten other inspiring people.

The fear has been felt. I've watched smiles of encouragement and shared in lots of laughter.

Each step each day was a little more challenging, each hour there was more resistance, and at the end of each day there was more pain! I pushed my body, mind, and soul to the limit, and I'm here. I survived with no blisters, just a bruised knee, and I'm rather proud of myself.

The sense of ultimate joy in my heart is immense: Beijing, the Great Wall of China, and the friends I have walked and talked with.

There is such beauty everywhere we go. When we open our eyes, there is beauty within our landscape, whether crumbling or renovated paths, a calm river to a fast-flowing waterfall, or the beauty of kindness shared when someone reaches out to you with their hand to support you.

So many hands have supported me over this last week as I worked each day conquering my fear of heights and learning more and accepting who I am and have become.

I have learned how to manage my centre of gravity when I descend, and I know I can trust myself to walk on the edge of high ridges and jump over and across rocks in a stream, and I can complete 400 very steep ascending steps and five days of trekking.

This adventure has taught me how to really challenge myself. And now as I sit here ready to leave, I'm reflecting on how far my personal journey is changing through my physical health, strength, and mental cultivation. I understand that I can do without everything (chocolate and cups of tea) I think I need.

My biggest lesson over these nine days was about my pace. I was always last and the slowest. In my twenties, I raced and did everything faster and harder to be the best and prove myself (to who?). It was another illusion.

I finally realised I have nothing to prove and to simply be. Each day, I am first in my world, and as I write this, I smile.

We are each a hero with our own story to live and tell. Be your hero.

Travel Zone

11 October 2010

Travel zone: That's what I'm in at the moment. I've been away from my own bed for four weeks, and I'm only two sleeps away from getting back in it.

Yesterday, I travelled back from Beijing, China, after spending nine days taking part in a charity challenge trek across five sections of the Great Wall. It was tough. After spending Sunday awake during an eleven-hour flight and two hours by train, I slept well. Today, I'm feeling the effects of both the time difference and the trek. My body and mind are all over the place – or should I say somewhere between China and the UK?

Travel does this, though. What I have done in the last week made me think about other travels, and only in the last three or four years have I relaxed about the whole travel thing.

We all love to travel. More so, it is often for a holiday and a chance to see family and friends, but how many of us still get frustrated about the travel experience? There's the packing, the cleaning the house before you leave (I still do this and still not sure why), the travel to the airport, flying, travel at the destination, accommodation, luggage, and then there's the part where we enjoy ourselves.

If I still travelled like I did those years ago, I don't think I would get anywhere. I've learned to enjoy the whole experience of traveling from the beginning to end. I'm the calm person in the queue at check in. I've learned over the years that I will always get a seat on a plane I am booked to travel on as long as I am in the queue at the right time. Always the same result.

A little planning of the trip removes all the stresses and unexpected huffs and puffs. I talk to many people when I'm travelling, and the most common thing I hear people say about their trips is that they do not enjoy being on the plane. For me, this is the best bit. Whilst in the air (at present), it is the only place I can be away from a mobile phone, Facebook, Twitter, and emails, and I have a choice if I want to watch a movie. It's a space I can just be without any guilt. With one more day left before I travel and less than twenty-four hours since my last journey, I'm packing my cases, getting ready to coming home, seeing my friends, and seeing the sea.

Crowded House

· ·

14 October 2010

I landed last night onto Cyprus soil tired and happy. In the last forty-eight hours, I had been up in the air for 16 of those. I've visited a city with around 21 million people living there, a vast difference from my home town of Paphos. From people swarming around, bicycles, cars and buses throwing out emissions, there was still an element of peace in such a busy bustling place.

The notes for the trip advised to retain a sense of humour. I only guess this is to help you with the immense number of people rushing by.

Where did the peace come from?

I'm sat here in my home now, and I can hear the birds chirping in the tree opposite my window. In the distance, there is the faint sound of a plane, and I can hear my fingers as they tap each key as I write.

Does peace come from awareness?

We live in a world with a lot of noise and distractions, and there is a fine line where chaos turns the volume up on the noise, and we lose our self-awareness. We lose our peace. Finding ways to turn down the noise and practicing them regularly helps us turn chaos into enjoyment each day. The pace, speed, people, and noise is all irrelevant to a degree. What you hold inside creates your peace and awareness.

We control the filters for our noise, so if you don't like what you are hearing, seeing, and feeling, we each can learn to accept, change, or move away from it. I wanted to experience and enjoy this new place, a city seeping in history, and I knew I would need to control the noise. I did. Finding our centre in a crowded house creates a peaceful experience. Breathing is the key to finding our centre.

From a crowded house with a mind filled with memories, I look to now and the peace in my home. It's great to be back.

West Coast Heaven?

16 October 2010

Is heaven on the west coast of Paphos with my own picture view?

Stepping out of Myrtle (my car) down at the beach, I felt an immediate spring in my step. Today was my first walk in a week.

No walking poles, no fabulous walking friends, no camera (broken in China), and no walking boots (left in UK to rest!). Back in my lighter cross trainers, I wonder if this is where my spring has sprung from.

The path I walk was modernised by the mayor a few years ago and stretches along towards Chloraka from the harbour. I started walking here four or so years ago when it was a rough track, and I would just sit when I reached the corner and watch the sea. Now I think it looks much like the yellow brick road, and yes, I guess I'm off to see the wizard! Each time I walk here, it becomes my time to create my dreams. It is my time to reflect, focus, and find my balance.

"The sea inspires me, let it take me away. Let it breathe with me and through me. I am the earth, the sun, the moon and the stars. I am the universe and I travel far." – Emma Lannigan

And more so now, it is a time for reflection. Yesterday, I noticed it was only eight weeks until my birthday, making Christmas ten weeks away and then New Year's.

We can all walk along the path forever; however, with vision, goals, and a plan, we can visit all the places we want to.

And that's what I now do each year. We can take control of what view we wish to see and what feelings we want to experience. This is a great time of year to start reviewing what you have achieved. Once you put pen to paper, you'll be surprised at just what you have achieved, no matter how big or small the experience. Each achievement leads you to your goal, your lifetime goals. Give yourself the chance to say, "Wow! I did all this. I *am* amazing!" You are. We are all too quick to criticise ourselves, when in fact, in five minutes, you can note down just how great we really are.

Walking for me was once for fitness. I would power walk for an hour a few times a week, and that would be my contribution to keeping me in check! It progressed into a way for me to relax, and I would walk, sit, and just simply be, watching and listening to each wave as it curled into the coast line. Walking became a challenge for my fitness and an opportunity to test myself in terms of commitment and focus ready to complete my charity trek. Now, I have to ask what walking means to me. I love walking for the time and space it creates. What is my motivation? Time and space.

West coast heaven? I think it is. This path is a sanctuary putting a spring in my step, revitalising and inspiring my mind, and relaxing and motivating me.

Do you have an equivalent heaven to retreat to? When you retreat, start reviewing your achievements this year and create your next moment now!

Adaptable

· ·

18 October 2010

One word with so many uses throughout our lives. To adapt is to be flexible and to vary routine, allowing creativity and for dreams to come true.

We can adapt immediately, physically, and mentally to overcome an obstacle or puzzle in the short, medium, and long term to achieve a goal.

Today, I'm embarking upon another lifestyle change. It's not a drastic one in terms of what I do. Rather, it's more in the way I am doing it. Life for the last twenty months has been without a regular routine or schedule, and today, I'm starting a new routine, adapting to supporting my next goal (in fact, it is the foundation of a few goals.)

In life, when we are certain, and I want to add positive, about something we want to achieve, things in our current world often require a little adjustment, which is perhaps why some people choose not to live their dreams. They are happy to accept what they are currently doing without making any changes.

We can be adaptable for only our own goals. Believing in your desires and yourself are the creation themselves. Accepting the changes to lifestyle, for instance, come as a blessing in support of your end outcome.

Knowing each step forward is heading to a destination you have chosen provides a sense of daily achievement, as each day you step closer. Within each day, any irritation, frustration, or anger is temporary. It's not real because you know in your heart that whatever today brings, it will always bring you closer to your goal.

It is the knowing and therefore the preparation in getting to your destination. Getting sidetracked and distracted will just delay the journey. It's your journey and destination, and the best way to get there is to enjoy it.

Your goal might be life changing or not, and each goal is important, regardless of impact. Each impact makes a difference. Each step takes you closer.

If we look at nature, nature is adaptable. The wind blows a tree, and the leaves rustle; a gale blows at the tree, and the tree changes shape. A river does not stop flowing; it has a continuous flow, from calm and soft to fast flowing down stream.

We are adaptable. We are part of nature, and nature is part of us. We only discover and trust just how much when we change our environment and are put to a challenge. There is no trickery in survival. We are only asked to accept the challenge and believe we will succeed.

Nature responds to its environment, and we have that choice, too. Inside our own world, we can close our eyes and know exactly how we wish to respond to our world. Close your eyes and ask how you will adapt to your day. Look at the things you dream of having, being, and doing. Are they happening? And if they are not, ask what you are doing to stop these happening? Listen for the answers.

With the answers, you always have the free will as to whether you want to adapt and make changes. If you don't, perhaps it wasn't really your goal. If this is the case, you can let it go. It will give you free space for something you do want to come into your life.

Be adaptable. Be amazing.

Changing View to Take a Break

....

19 October 2010

Working from home, the view from my office window can become just another thing that blends into the background. The only thing in view is my computer. The screen is pretty. I converted to an iMac over a year ago, and the main screen has a wonderful three-dimensional effect image of the stars with radiant light streams stretching the screen. However, we all need to take a break.

I write all day, starting in the morning on one topic. For the main part of the day, I write something else. Then in the evening, I write another blog. I love writing, and I have a great computer to do it on; however, we all need to take a break.

I've worked to create a life where I work from home. The office has not proven to be a supportive environment for me. I love the outdoors, fresh air, and walking, so having a balance to work and play is important for balance. For some (maybe you), working in an office environment supports your balance. The beauty is that we are all different. We have different needs and different wants. Wherever we choose to work though, we all need to build in time for a break.

The weather is awesome this time of year here on Cyprus, and I've been indoors, so I took myself out for a walk around the village, something I've not done since returning from the UK. I love this village. From my veranda, I can see the sea, and the sun was burning brightly reflecting what appeared to be gold in front of my eyes. I popped on my trainers and my iPod, selected my coaching playlist (thirty-seven personally selected tracks that are happy, motivational, and inspiring; I'll share with you someday), and started my needed break.

Walking through the older streets of the village is heart-warming; the character and tradition can just be felt everywhere. With my songs and dancing spirit, to anyone passing me, they would have noticed I was actually dancing as I was walking. Today, I didn't care. I'm happy. I smiled at ladies sitting at the front of their houses after a moment of hesitation. When they smiled back, it was great. I wonder how many people walk by and don't bother to smile. They were simply taking their needed break.

Circling round at the top of the village, this part is my favourite. There today, was a view of pure grace, untouched nature, a picture just for me, the golden sun, setting on the horizon casting an immense golden glow across the tranquil sea. Here was my break.

Energised, refreshed, and rested. Take a needed break. Our body and mind work much better with a clear mind and relaxed body.

Give: With Random Kindness

....

19 October 2010

I was travelling back to the UK to start my journey to China. Landing in London Gatwick Airport I had to make the trains back to home first. So heading off right into the heart of the city to King's Cross train station, I was packed for a four-week trip, carrying my rucksack and two suitcases, all amounting to somewhere around forty kilograms. It was heavy even by my standards!

So after finding the lift at Gatwick, I raced to make my connecting train. So far so good with a trolley to help. However, after the ticket window, the trolley had to be parked, and from the journey onwards, it was just me and these bags. Boarding the train from here until Victoria, I knew I could rest. For what happened I didn't expect would.

Off at Victoria, I had to make it across the concourse to the underground, manoeuvring other passengers. Ticket in hand and place in the gate, I managed to walk through. Now how was I going to get down the escalator with all my luggage? Not thinking, I just threw a bag across my back and my rucksack and then balanced the other suitcase next to me. I literally prayed the weight would not throw me forward.

Onto the tube and next stop King's Cross. With a new layout, I couldn't find the lift, and time was pressing for the 20.30 train. Heading for the stairs, stopping just at the bottom to prepare to throw the bag once again on my shoulder, I heard an angel's voice. "Can I take that for you?" Without chance to reply, the man was carrying the bag to the top, and once at the top, he was gone as quickly as he arrived, slightly embarrassed that he'd helped someone, or the surprise at how heavy it was!

All the same, I was very grateful. Although for days after the journey, my body ached.

Returning home, I had decided to fly from a different airport, choosing Birmingham, the same distance by train and no tube journeys, just one station change. This trip, five kilograms lighter, started very well with my brother in law carrying one of the bags over the stairs at the rail station. There was relief the journey was to start with no pain. There was only one concern on this journey and that was at the changing-over station, where I recalled there were more stairs and that I hadn't seen lifts. It would be okay, and I'd just have to work it out when I got there.

Into my journey, I became aware that one of my bags was in the way and changed seats to keep it in view. Opposite the aisle was a gentleman who seemed to be working on papers, and I settled and decided to continue staring out the window, to keep awake. The end of the line and all change. I got up, put on my rucksack, and had both bags at my feet, stepping to the side of the doors to let this same gentleman through, he asked, "Can I help you with this?"

He carried the bag to the platform and asked where I was going. I explained and accepted his help. He replied, "It's OK I'll take it to the top." Off we both walked up the stairs with my luggage. He continued walking with me and towards information where I needed to check what platform it was for the connecting train. When we had arrived at the top of the stairs for my platform I stopped and asked, "Are you going this way?"

He replied, "No, but at least I have done my act of kindness today!"

He certainly had, I thought, as he walked to the platform, set down the case, and shook my hand with a smile.

I boarded my next train, arrived, collected a trolley, and went straight to check in. Journey complete. A happy lady, and I guess a happy gentlemen for knowing he had helped someone that day.

People are often afraid to help strangers, thinking they might be interfering, or they might be told their help is not needed. If you can manage the rejection, offer your help, because the chances are the person you help will be so very grateful.

The chance of you being helped is quite likely that you are willing to help others as kindness attracts kindness.

Be random and act in kindness today, tomorrow, and every day. belifehappy.

Love: Your Light

. . . .

21 October 2010

"You've been provided with a perfect body to house your soul for a few brief moments in eternity. So regardless of its size, shape, colour, or any imagined infirmities, you can honour the temple that houses you by eating healthfully, exercising, listening to your body's needs, and treating it with dignity and love." – Dr Wayne Dyer

Welcome to this amazing moment. A moment you created. Create all your moments today from love. Love is your source of life, and it is abundantly held within you and surrounds you. Love is formed as light, and we each have our own lever to control our light. For when it ever becomes dark, you can remember the light within you and turn your lever up. Create the light in your day.

We are each blessed with a powerful mind and body and yet they fall and weaken to disease when we get too complex with them. They both work well when the mind and body is rested and relaxed and when the body is fed with simple, noncomplex food.

You can use your light to become so bright that only good and positive people, messages, and environments are seen and experienced by you. It is not to become ignorant of life, simply to manage and control the balance of the positive and negative in our life.

It is all within our balance, to manage the darkness and the light within friendships, relationships, our families, our work, and our life.

Joy will be in each day when we all open our hearts and let our light guide us, inspiring our dreams. We each have an immense purpose and reason for our presence. This is an ultimate gift we hold within ourselves. When we are in our own space and time, we can close our eyes and feel this purpose. We do not need to see or hear it in our waking conscious minds. Just knowing you have an immense purpose for being here is an incentive to live each day, glowing in our light of love.

Share this light. Be blessed you are an angel of earth, and your wings protect and love everyone around you. You are safe. Take this love today. Wrap it up, and put it in your pocket, or your purse.

be love. be life happy.

Orchestra of Hidden Treasures

• •

25 October 2010

There are lots of hidden treasures everywhere we go, and I'm not talking about places of interest. Instead, I'm talking about people.

Each person we come across has a wonderful hidden treasure and provides an opportunity for us to learn, listen, give support, laugh, and love. A balance is surely about all of these things, and delightfully, my weekend has been filled with all.

In the chaos of earthbound life, it is easy to forget how everyone around us and involved in our life is a reflection of what and who we are. For instance, if you work in a shop, the people around you each day will be in the main customers. The interaction you have will be what you create when you welcome the customers in the door or at the counter. This is the same for every situation we are in, and bringing the balance in is the fun part. It's where you conduct your orchestra of hidden treasures.

One by one, as you intend to create each day with an open mind and to focus on the present moment, the people in your life become each present moment. As it is experienced, it feels like a gift, and it looks to be an illusion. It's incomprehensible or coincidence, and we hear the question in our mind, "How did this happen?"

The people in our lives are miracles we created. At times, we might have a negative experience with a partner, family member, or friend. Instead of allowing the frustration, anger, and upset to creep into this situation and your life, allow yourself to ask the magic question of why. It can look like a puzzle when we start to ask why, like a key part of the orchestra is missing. To find it, think about what is happening in your life at this present time. Why would a negative situation occur? What have you been ignoring in your life? Is there a message in the situation you can learn from?

When we learn and make choices from our experiences, we grow, and we find more hidden treasures. You then have your full orchestra. The music is harmonic, and your life is in balance.

What hidden treasures have you overlooked? Be guided to stay in the present moment, and watch the people who enter your life today, from the people you live with to the people you work with or pass by in the supermarket or the street. What gift will your give them to add to their orchestra? We are each orchestrating our own harmonic music to create one beautiful sound.

Share your hidden treasure, and allow your unique sound to reflect your beautiful light.

Give: An Inspired Lesson

. . . .

26 October 2010

We all like to help others and give to others. Through friendship, relationships, and our work, we share laughter, tears, love, achievement, encouragement, a helping hand, our experiences, and what we have learned along the way.

It is not surprising, though some lessons are left for us to encounter on our own, and we might share these with others when we have learned our lesson. It's important to add there is no race, either. We will each encounter exactly what we are meant to, some more than others, and of course in different and in similar ways.

The interesting lesson in giving is exactly that giving. We've heard giving and receiving are the balance, the ying and yang of life, and in keeping the balance, it helps our mind and body remain in balance. Therefore, we give and receive optimum health. When do we know whether we have given too much or too little? Is there too much or too little? The answer always comes back to the balance, and we each have our own ways of learning what the imbalance warning signs are.

With mind and body (and spirit) working, or more so knitting away together our life, and each moment, they are aware when the imbalance starts – with one of them slowing down to set off a warning sign. When the first warning sign is sent and it is not received, another is sent. Each warning may be subtle and easy to go unnoticed in a busy life or a busy person. It can become the background ache in our body, discomfort in the stomach, a sore throat, or the cold that will not go away. With everything we do not see, if we are meant to, it will come back, so another warning is sent. This time, it is to make sure the owner occupying takes notice.

It's here we have choices. Why am I experiencing this? When was the last time I experienced this? What was going on in my life then that is similar to now? Or, we can simply say it's okay. I'll get better soon. And we do, until the next time.

It's a hard idea to grasp. Our mind and body are there to support us on this journey, and the warning signs are there for a reason. We each have been given a gift of trust and intuition. We know deep down what we are required to do, and the answer comes without fear. Fear keeps the symptoms.

Giving too much sometimes can be found when we look at what we do. How do others around you view you? The key question is how many times do you say yes, especially to things we might not really want to do? (And that's not because you don't have the time; it's simply because you don't want to.)

I ask you with your kind heart to remember to be kind to yourself. Giving is a wonderful gift; however, it will no longer be a gift when you are not able to give it because you have not given to yourself. It's okay to ask for help and to offer help. Always offering to help and not asking means you will be out of balance.

There are enough of us to give and receive, and we can do this in so many ways. Each small action of kindness you give creates a big help to someone else.

Just remember to keep yourself in the cycle. belifehappy.

Love: Inside Out

· ·

28 October 2010

We spend the majority of our time looking outside, with everything coming to us from the outside. It can feel like chaos is surrounding us until we find time to go inside.

Inside, we find peace. At the beginning, when we first find this place, it feels alien and an uncomfortable peace. There's no one special place we are required to create or go to; where you are now is space enough for you to love inside.

The peace you find is the feeling of your body relaxing, sinking into itself, leaving worries, stress and aches and pains behind. Inside, there is no pain, simply peace. Your mind becomes free, and awareness becomes focused on a different view from inside. In this relaxed state, you are at peace, and you are resting your body and mind, energising them both for whatever you do next. This time is precious in our thinking. It separates the chaos outside and the peace within. It helps us create and maintain a balance point and a safe place to retreat and relax in.

We all need this peace to function at our best, to be creative, and to express our love. In our relaxed state, we learn about our outside world, and we can use the peace to be creative and to be aware of ourselves and our surroundings. We begin to feel our environment, and we feel our thoughts. With each visit inside, we learn how our thoughts are our feelings and actions. We take this to the outside and watch how we make more precise decisions, decisions that feel and sound right. The time inside allows us on the outside to express ourselves in a way we might not have been aware of before. This helps us communicate our intentions and getting the results we are looking for in our life.

To visit the inside is free, and in return for our time, we are rewarded with the gift of peace, joy, harmony, love, and the awareness and growth from being inside to create the outside. Love inside out.

Poem

Peace within draws a light,
With each visit day or night,
The light simmers, flickers, and grows,
Until over the days, months, and years, we know,
The light takes flight, reaching far and wide,
Reaching up to the skies, invisible of course to the human eye,
This light becomes a floating mist, soothing, like a kiss,
Touching each of our human souls,
Protecting each step, and guiding us with love, to our goals.

be love. be light. be life. be happy. belifehappy.

Time

1 November 2010

For me, in the last two days, time has moved more into my awareness, and from it, I have learned a pattern in my world. It is not to be broken or changed, simply for me to be accepted and rejoice in this gift.

Time. Children often do this, and I wouldn't like to think I especially placed my parents in deep discomfort (or my sister) as my most often asked question was, "What is the time?" As children, we don't have the same concept of time as adults, we don't have knowledge of what is to come, and we're not in a race as such except for curiosity. We learn to read the time, and of course, time became part of me. Me and Mickey Mouse.

Watching my grandpa eat at Christmas, he was exceptionally slow. However, he always appeared to enjoy each moment. Eating dinner or not, he took life at a pace he was comfortable with. He observed his surroundings and always looked to be smiling.

I was and still am slow at eating. I love food and enjoy the taste and the social company. I like to stroll, stop, and observe what is around me. I love to smile inside and out. I choose to enjoy time.

When I experienced depression ten years ago, I felt I had no time. When people asked me about doing things, there was simply no time. I was so busy, except I wasn't. I was an empty shell burning more calories than I was putting in as I had no time for anything: talking, washing my hair, or eating.

I've already mentioned earlier how I observed my pace in China and how it had upset me to a degree that I was slower than most of the group. I was also slow at eating dinner. This was all my perception.

So over the last month or so, I've been unconsciously assessing and evaluating my time. I looked at how I use it and what pace my time is. Being very flexible, I feel no need to change, as change is part of my life. I am, however, in the process of accepting my pace in life. My pace of doing is my pace of being and having. If I choose to speed up the pace, I am in control of that. When I am allowing other external factors to control my speed, I eventually feel uneasy.

Our vision of life changes, and with it, we each bring the flexibility of our choice for mental and physical balance, which creates ease. To everything we do, be, and have, we control our pace. On my evaluation, I do not do anything fast (apart from writing and typing). Everything else is at a pace I control and manage. When I am in control and managing my world, everyone in my world benefits. This is my lesson. This is what I am accepting.

With rushes of anticipation, we must prepare to have many; otherwise, we will feel loss in our time. To manage our work (daily life) at a consistent pace, we maintain our inner and outer balance of the world.

Be in your time. Choose your time, and share your time. Your world is never waiting; it is always within you.

Bring Light into Winter

· ·

2 November 2010

Those nights are sure drawing in. It's five-thirty in the evening, and I'm all over the place, feeling hungry. I'm now starting to think my body clock is set by daylight and the position of the sun rather than the clock. Darkness. It's not really got a happy tone to it; however, here more than many places in the world, we have such a positive reason to use our daylight and our dark hours to fantastical purposes. Wouldn't you agree?

This morning was a prime example (although a shocking first in my nearly thirty-four years). I woke early at six-thirty to no alarm and suddenly realised I could get up now, get out, and go for a run to the beach and walk back. By seven-fifteen, I was home stretching and putting the kettle on. So the first is the running. I've walked, power-walked, cycled, and swam – not running!

I'm looking for some energy to shake me up and keep me active in the darker months, and walking isn't ideal and is difficult to fit in after work. It's not a new concept to many; however, I enjoy my eight hours sleep, so getting up early to make the most of the daylight is new to me. With the clocks changing, I seemed quite awake and ready to just go for it. Get out there in the early morning light, and shake myself up for the day. How did I feel? Awesome! It was to the point that I think my friend staying with me was quite alarmed at my alertness and happiness at such an hour.

Making the most of the natural daylight is a mood booster - a natural mood booster. It was at university in my final year, while writing my dissertation, I was introduced to light and mood enhancement. I was feeling sluggish and low, and my lecturer had noticed. He could have just ignored how I was feeling, however instead he made a suggestion that I started switching on lights in the morning during the winter months. It really made a difference. He then suggested I went home for a week during the holidays - a change and more chance of being outside back at home. Light, fresh air; simple, natural and yet so effective.

Turn up your natural light, breathe and bring more light into your day.

Give: What Size is Your Stress?

2 November 2010

Stress comes in many shapes and sizes. How big is your stress today? Go back ten years, and ask the person next to you how they felt or what they thought about stress. Their answer is more likely to be negative and unhelpful. Today, stress is recognised as an effect on the mind and body. For years, it's been promoted, and most of you will be aware now that stress can be good or bad. (I don't like that word!) That's why I'm asking you now to ask yourself:

- How big is your stress today?
- What does your stress feel like?
- How does it make you feel?
- Where do you feel your stress in your body if you could locate it?
- What would happen if you changed what you were doing to create a less stressful outcome?

Stress is a chemical reaction of the endocrine system (hormones), and stress is created from our adrenal glands, creating the fight-or-flight syndrome. To fight is to be in a competitive situation, one where winning is the end goal. This is positive in sport and games, and the very same effect on the body is produced when we fight ourselves in stressful situations. What is overlooked is the effects the repeated fights have on our body and mind. What starts as stress develops as further imbalance in the mind and body, creating illness and leading to long-term effects of depression to heart disease. During the fight or flight, our heart rate increases, sending blood around our bodies faster, energising our muscular system, and slowing the systems that are not required, such as the digestive and urinary system. In a sense, in a fight-or-flight situation, we are blinkered towards the stress just as our body has aligned to support the mind.

Our body and mind respond all the time in fight or flight (competition or fear.) Where there is a negative, there will be a positive.

If we can choose stress, we can also choose it's opposite: to relax. In a relaxed state, the mind and body repair itself, sending blood to all parts, at a steady pace, removing waste and providing nutrients to the skin. A relaxed body has a wonderful healthy glow.

Now there's a balance. We each require a feeling of get up and go. Our fight-or-flight system is also there as a protective system in times when we really need to run and in times when we are at play. However, as with everything, balance comes.

There are people who love adrenalin and live healthy exhilarating lives, and they do so through their balance. They know how to relax. (You might not see them do it, but they do.) There are those people who live very busy lives and are always against the clock. They don't relax, burn out, and end up feeling forced to change careers, which inevitably changes their whole life.

So what's this relaxing about? How do we know if we are relaxing? Ask yourself. Pay attention to how your body feels. Pay attention to the words you are choosing to use? How do the words sound and feel to you? So many questions, and ultimately we are the only one person who really knows whether we are creating time to relax.

Pay attention to you, and stop stress controlling you.

Play: Stressless

3 November 2010

Tense, sweaty palms, fast pulse? Let's look at turning the effects of stress around with this simple and very effective gift we all have.

Poem

How big is your stress? Does your stress fit you?

Is it too short, too tall,
Too big, too small,
Too thick, too thin,
Not sure where to begin?

Does the sweat in your palm cause you alarm?
Sat in your meeting room,
Do you hear your heart going, boom, BOOM?

Inside, you are racing,
Your mind tracing,
The past the future – all at once,
Preparing to fight or was that flight,
You can only be sure with one thing in sight.

A stop sign, the end,
Just at the bend,
A chance to change direction,

From relaxing and inward inspection.
You know it's time to put an injection
Of love and balance,
Into the mix,
With now, no time for tricks.

A good night's sleep,
Something to eat,
The pleasures all missed in the race.

All at once, you can slow ... your ... pace,
And now you can look and see your glowing illuminated face.

Written by Emma Lannigan

Exercise

Wherever you feel stress, let the gift of your breathing relax you
there, right *now*.

Place one hand on your stomach, and relax the other. If you are
standing in a queue, for example, keep your back straight and relax
your body from your hips. Just feel from straightening yourself that
you already feel calmer. Now, with your hand on your stomach,
take a deep breath in. No one needs to know what you are doing.
Take the breath through your nose, a long inward inhalation drawing
the breath deep into your stomach. Your hand will feel your breath
reach your stomach. Then slowly exhale, through your mouth. Keep
exhaling until you have exhaled all. Then repeat at least three times.

The focus of your intention on your breath will distract your mind and
body from the stress you were experiencing. You will feel calmer and
more in control of what you are doing.

Breathing techniques like that above are great to help those people who don't sleep very well. Again, from the focus and intention of breathing, you forget why you are not able to sleep. All you needed was a relaxed mind and body.

Once in a calm state, affirmations help the mind focus and maintain the calm you have achieved through breathing. An affirmation can be any positive statement that helps you; however, here are some examples:

I am strong, confident, and successful.
I am happy, at peace, and loved.
I am in control of X situation.
I am achieving my targets of X today.

Affirmations begin with "I am" as it communicates to ourselves that we are already in this state; 'Act as if" statements. They are positive, and in a repeated positive state, we begin to act out what we are telling ourselves.

I am an amazing individual!

(Yes you are!)

Use the gift of breathing we were given, and remind yourself with your gift of words that you are doing and being everything you are supposed to be doing right now.

Third Time Lucky?

....

4 November 2010

In the past five years, I've moved to Cyprus three times, so is this third time lucky? On this week's anniversary of the last move, I realise I am home. That's a start.

Balancing life starts with birth and ends in death, and the bit in the middle – well, with the positive, you will experience the negative. Balance is simply the key. This week has sent so many messages to me about the life I'm living at the moment and my futuere goals. The only thing stopping me moving into the future is the past.

Nearly three years ago, I left this island, my friends, my job, my apartment, and my car and took off back to the UK after my dad died suddenly. It seemed the right thing to do, to be home in familiar surroundings with lifelong friends. It was a good move. It gave me time to think and process what had happened. Access to bereavement counselling and a routine life kept me focused.

I took the time to retrain, starting with reiki, holistic massage, and NLP coaching. I stopped smoking twenty a day, and with all my learning, I changed my interests and social scene. I became a nonstop learning machine, reading endless books and meditating religiously. When what I wanted to do came to an end, I had known for a while that I wanted to return 'home.' The UK wasn't my home anymore. It was my family's home, but it just not mine anymore. My home was in Cyprus. I moved back a year ago this week. It was the third time I've moved here, so my question is whether it is third time lucky.

A lot of emotions have been stirring this week. What have I achieved in being back here? What are my plans now? I always have an underlying plan, my guide, I guess, to my life. It helps me make decisions because I already know what I want and don't want. This is good. I can move forward.

As with the end of any chapter, we always look back. That's okay to review. When I woke up with a grumpy grey cloud over my head, was this an excuse for something I'm not facing? The reality is that we cannot move forward until we let go of the past and accept and learn from it. Whilst I know my dad is no longer living, I'm not able to accept it. That's the truth, and how does the saying go? "Truth hurts."

The island is my balance. It's my home, and whilst this year has seen me swing from the high to the low frequently, inside in my heart, I know where to find my peace. My next task is to find my life balance and accept and learn from the past. I always have right now. I always have the horizon on my doorstep, watching the morning and evening skies and the deep blue winter sea. I've just realised that I am a fire sign. I live right next to water. There's my balance!

Love: Dissolves Stress

· ·

4 November 2010

Love dissolves everything. It universally has no judgment and is exactly what the word says, feels, and sounds like.

Then there is the perception of love. Here we're feeling the unconditional love that holds no questions or answers. It simply is.

As our external world builds ever more with increasing numbers and ratios of people experiencing stress, there is also another world that is increasingly building the power of universal love. Looking at this as a set of balancing scales, the stress is weighing heavier right now across the world; it will, however, not take long for love to balance the stress.

Many of us (at least one in four) have been stressed and experience a form of mental illness, and I wonder if there is a statistic that says how many in ten have found love. Although both stress and love are perceptional feelings; only the individual can measure.

For decades, feelings have been suppressed or ignored in order to achieve. It was as though the illusion of life became one of robotics with a series of functional stages and things we must achieve on the way to being socially acceptable. What has been suppressed for many years is now reawakening. People have become disillusioned with the stages and want to discover more. They want more from their life in terms of experiences, and to experience, we feel, and when we feel, we understand love.

We have become used to wrapping ourselves up in a tense coat, like body armour, to face another day. There is more suppression of where and who we want to be and be doing. Letting go of our amour is to experience the weight lifting from us, and a lighter, brighter day welcoming you.

Choose what you want to achieve from your day, work, relationships, and health. It seems a large task, and it is: It's your life. Today is the day and the moment that requires your focus. So as with everything, your vision and thoughts create the weight of your jacket. By making a start on what you'd realistically like from a situation and focusing on that, the likely outcome is that you will achieve it. It wasn't a miracle or a coincidence. Rather, you created. You deserve the praise!

For the little time in the planning of your vision, you can wake each day and focus on just today. Each day is a step in the feeling of new trainers, soft and bouncy. Stress is caused by losing control of our life. Get your control back, and there are some great ways to support yourself.

The more love we experience, the less stress we experience. As the saying goes, love conquers all.

be love. be life. be happy. belifehappy.

Immense Gratitude

7 November 2010

Where else can you get the immense feeling of gratitude than when you feel you are in the right place at the right time feeling fabulously right?

Yesterday, after a lovely relaxing afternoon on my veranda reading, I headed off to my favourite spot to join the yellow brick road. I was planning on a little stroll, but as I looked around and saw all the other people, couples, tourists, and individuals running, power walking, and strolling, I felt motivated and added a spring into my step.

My time was absent, and the red burning sun in the sky just above the horizon was my only guide. The sky awash with pink candy floss clouds. I could have easily been in sweet heaven!

I sat down in my own window box. Placing my feet firmly on the wooden floor, I felt myself ground and connect with the earth. Above, I felt myself sit upright, the feeling of my crown being pulled upward to the skies. In front of my eyes was the most beautiful sunset. Behind it a new moon was rising. I was surrounded and connected to the sky, the earth, the sun, and the moon. I did feel that everything outside of me, as well as time, was absent. I was there. In that moment. I was connected. The sun marbled with yellow, orange, and red, and I thought I could see the energy moving within it until it had gone. Just for today.

Shaking myself off, I set to return home, this time not only with a spring in my step and also a smile on my face reflecting my inner peace. After a busy week and morning, those five minutes of being brought me back to the present and a state of peace.

When We Ask, Do They Listen?

8 November 2010

Angels have been a strong theme for me this weekend. They have been a strong theme in my life since I walked into a bookstore in 2008 heading for the *Alchemist* and then dropping my eye to see *How to Hear your Angels* by Doreen Virtue staring at me. More recently, in the last week, a friend gave me a book named *Spirit Guides and Angel Guardians* by Richard Webster, saying I might be interested. So this weekend, I started to read it.

As my life transformed a few years back, so did my friends. The mentioning of angels in conversation does make some people uncomfortable. However, as with a lot of things reawakening now, so too is the belief in angels. If we ask, will they listen? Will they answer our prayers?

Through research, I have learned that belief is the key. It's not the secret, the law of attraction, or religiously aligned. The only alignment the belief needs is to be aligned with the person asking. You could say, whether you ask through prayer, thought, or angels, someone is listening.

Is this too much to imagine there is someone, an angel, guardian angel, archangel, or God, listening and acting on our thoughts and prayers?

Have you ever before gone to do something for someone and just asked aloud or in your head for what you would like to happen – in other words, your desired outcome? What happened?

Have you heard the story about the car driver always getting the same perfect parking space when he goes to the supermarket by simply asking? Have you experienced this?

Is this your guardian angel listening and answering your thoughts?

It still comes back to personal belief. They will only be your guardian angels if you let them know you are happy to have them in your life.

I've found the angels to be a great source of comfort and daily guidance to me, and I refer to daily angel cards for their great source of inspiration, love, and motivation. They are also a great way to practice daily kindness, gratitude, and the reminder to experience joy.

So are they listening, and whom am I asking?

The word *angel* means messenger, and the –el, which comes from the end of the archangels' names, mean *shining being*. I read this in wonder as my initials are EL.

Archangel Michael, named one who is like God, is the most familiar of angels; he represents love and can be called upon to help protect you.

Archangel Gabriel can be called upon to overcome doubt and fear.

Archangel Raphael can be called upon for healing (emotionally and physically).

Archangel Uriel can be called upon for clear thinking.

There are other angels and of course your own guardian angels. You can ask for whomever you think of or remember; for those who truly require help and guidance, it is never a case of getting the wrong number. The message will be passed on, and you will receive the help you asked for.

You ask, believe, and receive. (And show gratitude.)

There is never a time you are alone. You are always in the comfort of your angels. They teach you and work with you to fulfil this lifetime journey in the way you intended it to be. There are only benefits to working with the angels in your daily life; this one, however, is one I know happened to me. At the time, though, I didn't know. Within the first year of my transformation, I would see people in the village or at the supermarket, and they would say, "Wow don't you look amazing you have such a wonderful glow!" And I did. I felt amazing and light. I felt the abundance of love, health, and joy in my life.

Do they always listen? Yes, which is why you will have read many times here how your thoughts create reality, so what you are thinking now is effectively creating the next moment.

So what are you thinking?

Just when you are about to lose faith – you asked, you believed, and you received – and then you changed your mind? Be focused on what you ask for. Be thankful for what you ask for, and there are no limits to how many times you ask for help.

You can believe in angels or believe in stars. Each one will guide you far.

This week, what will you be asking for? Now believe (see, feel, hear, and be) and receive it with gratitude. Enjoy!

Give: Easing the Festive Pressure

....

9 November 2010

It's about this time of year when there is much gratitude paid through Remembrance Day and Thanksgiving. This time of year also brings with it the colder months and the building pressure of Christmas.

It's a busy time, and through TV commercials and email newsletters, we're constantly reminded of what we must be buying or should have on our Christmas lists. Do you feel the pressure?

It's easy for us all to fall into this trap. Why would we not want our Christmas to be the best, with our family we love, our partners, and the wonderful exchange of gifts and bountiful feast? Do you feel the pressure?

What do you give thanks for? What will the two-minute silence on 11 November at eleven in the morning mean to you? What does Christmas feel like? What is Christmas about for you? And how do we wrap up kindness? We haven't seen kindness sold on our TVs, and how can anyone sell kindness? The true beauty of kindness is that it comes from a person's heart. Its value is priceless.

Whilst buying and exchanging gifts is a symbol of your kindness, showing and offering help to those around you who are feeling the pressure at this time of year, is a greater kindness. There's something not right about Christmas tipping the balance over to debt to create happiness for one day. The smallest gift wrapped with thought and kindness has a far greater value than an expensive price tag and no thought.

Today, tomorrow, and every day, give thought and kindness and share your value with your world. You are the ultimate gift in your life, and in exchange, you share your light.

Be aware of the pressure, slow down, and enjoy the coming weeks with thanks. belifehappy.

Change and Perspective

....

11 November 2010

We all know there is no certainty in life except change. Everything is changing, everything is moving, and yet we are always surprised and shocked when things do happen. I've been looking for (or perhaps asking for) some things in my life to happen, and I have to say I'm feeling very grateful as they start to happen. More so, I'm aware they are happening.

I moved into a lovely place at the end of March. I could even go so close to saying that it is perfect – for me. The space, the surroundings, and the peace it brings all make for a lovely feeling. It's home. Workwise, at the end of the summer, things were not going at all to plan, and my focus was shifting heavily on my fundraising. Honestly, I didn't know if I would be able to stay here, but this is my home, and more than anything, I wanted to keep it. My prayers have been answered, and here I am, happily typing from the comfort of my home.

So whilst my security needs look to be balancing, my foundations took a shake in the wake of the news that a lovely, bright, and happy lady had passed away. This lady was in her prime of life, which of course made me think right now about whether I am who I want to be and doing all that I want to do. Another friend passed away earlier this year, and her death also gave me a shake in where I was.

I have been wondering what to do for Christmas regarding gifts and postage and cards and gifts. And then, right before me, was perspective.

Somehow, everything that mattered does not, and everything just is.

Earlier today, as I was in the supermarket picking up chocolate, something caught my eye that made me smile: a Santa mug and Santa tea light holder. They are so much fun, and today they just reminded me that life is now. Life is the value I place on it. Today is precious.

To achieve balance, I read we must be willing to change and experience new things, and we must focus on all key areas of our life. By just focusing on one, we will be successful in that area but unbalanced in the others. This is me. I have achieved the balance in my health after my trip and in my work, which ultimately will reward me, and it now leaves me with relationships, an area I've left out of focus for a very long time. I ask myself a question each day: "If today is TODAY, have I achieved everything I want to, and am I happy?" When the answer is no, then I know what it is time to do: change it.

Circle and a Smiley Face

. . . .

15 November 2010

Is what makes life appear difficult at times that we are each responsible for our own health, happiness, love, and knowledge? What about the acceptance of there being no blame and no excuses?

Welcome ease, and allow yourself to affirm:

I am in control of my health, happiness, love, relationships, and learning.

I am. You are. Now.

Looking outside through your front window or kitchen window, what you are seeing will have some impact on your thoughts and feelings about today. You can choose how you feel. Ultimately, it's an illusion, which in a positive way, allows the day to become whatever you would like it to be – happy, with warmth and joy, versus dull, boring, and depressive.

Most of my work is with people, the ways they communicate, and the ways they can restore balance in their mind and body. The most important simple message to share with them is how the mind and body do not work alone, and this is a visualisation I shared with a client last week who was feeling a little under the weather. It is a great way for you to start your new week.

Exercise

Create an image in your mind of a circle, and now bring the circle to life by adding a smiley face.

Now picture your body, from head to toe, filled with these smiley faces. Take note of any frowns and change them to smiles.

Are they all smiling?

Really smiling?

How big are their smiles?

Can you make the smiles bigger?

How bright are they?

Can you make them brighter?

Are you smiling?

Are you now?

Friend (ships)

. . . .

16 November 2010

This past week, I would not have made through (sanely and in health) without my friends. Each is uniquely special, each with a different view in my guidance. It's just what I need. The theme of my conversations, not realising my unconscious has been busy suppressing some huge emotion, is ultimately my now greatest fear is of being on my own – you know, like for life.

Jumping right back to now. Here. I am single. I have been for over three years now, and here's the thing: I've lived on my own for seven years. I'm independent (except for DIY) with what some describe as a strong mind. I don't want my life to stand still too long, which is why I moved to Paphos in the first place. Life was stagnant. Yes, I had a great job and benefits – the company car; pension; and other plans for this, that, and the other. The glowing reality was right there that this was all I had. I had no partner, lived on my own, and had no hobbies. Life was a monotonous cycle of work, Tesco, home, dinner, TV, TV dinner, and bed. On the weekends, I'd break out, go binge drinking, and then do a two-hour walk – my version of past balance!

I was twenty-eight, and now (ouch) six years on, things are very different except for one thing: this fear of being on my own. Right back to now. I love my life. I have my freedom, wonderful and amazing friends who make me laugh and smile, and I have so many amazing interests like walking and writing. I have balance. I have peace.

The reality hits when you know you are not the only one who has a thing – we all do. We are all human, with emotions, all processing at different times and spaces. It's our friends who help us through these things. They make us cups of tea, cook us dinner, share their kindness, become a shoulder as our eyes leak, listen as we attempt to make sense of where we are and what to do, slow us down when we become panicked, and give us a hug we can't get anywhere else.

We all have wonderful friends. I'm very blessed to have a handful of very special friends in my life, some not in the same country as me. However, all the same, they (we) know when we need each other. No questions to ask – just to be there. As for my dear friends here, as one mentioned this week, "you really are on your own here... you must talk to your friends, we're always here." Living away from our first home, back in the UK, did we take for granted our friendships or even understand the depths and amazing fulfilment there is in friendships? Not just for shopping or going to the pub, either. Friends help you through the absolute rough and the blissfully smooth, because no matter what, there are no questions asked.

Our friendships change and move on, just as we do. Welcoming new people into our lives makes our journey that much more rewarding with new knowledge and places to go. They are always in your life, lifetime friends. They might not be right by your side, or to talk to every day or once a month even, but these friends have no time limit. They are always there.

Whether you need a boat or plane to see your friends or can walk round the corner or drive to the next village, our friends are who we are, wherever we are. Have fun, pick up the phone, laugh lots, and send your love.

Give: No Separation

16 November 2010

There is no separation of your mind, body, or spirit. When you wish to proceed in your life, we are required to be at one with ourselves, meaning your mind, body, and spirit are all in agreement with your direction.

Each of us works on a stronger level than perhaps someone we know; however, as we step forward on our journey, we bring and recognise all parts. The universe is whole. There is no separation.

It is therefore important to remain in the cycle when giving: to give and to forgive and to do this internally and externally. There are times when we are required to forgive ourselves for something in the past. We can spend years fighting events that may have occurred back in childhood; however, there becomes a time when we are presented again with the choice of forgiveness or anger and sadness.

There is no separation in forgiveness, as it is us as a whole who requires forgiveness and also the forgiveness of the situation. The focus is learning from the events and emotions and accepting them in order to acknowledge our forgiveness.

As a result, these events can be immense and life-changing, and it can be very daunting to face them and acknowledge that we are still experiencing anger and sadness from them. However, when you place yourself in the all of your mental, physical, and spiritual self, you become stronger, you can face these emotions, and start your process of forgiveness.

In this process, you are making way to give yourself a new experience in life. By holding on to limiting and negative emotions, we hold ourselves back from similar life situations that could enhance.

Forgiveness requires commitment and focus to let go whilst remaining as one. The pain as the emotions release is temporary – it is a release. It is similar to your internal healing system. Releasing the negative emotions leaves you feeling as though a shift has occurred.

The shift is your gift, much like a key to a door you wanted so much to open and would not. With the emotions released, you will open that door and the light welcoming you is awesome. It is a gift like no other, a part of your life you didn't think you could ever know.

For your work and forgiveness, you will be given the greatest gift.

Giving to ourselves is sometimes the answer to removing internal blocks stopping the things you want in your life coming in. Free your blocks, and open your door.

be one. be love. be light. be life. be happy. belifehappy.

Love: Two Parts Make a Whole

18 November 2010

"Marriage is the union of two souls joined in love, mutual respect, and commitment. It signifies as desire to deepen love over time. Your wedding day is a testament to your well-founded faith in love's power. Continually breathe life into that faith and love. Dearest One." – Daily Guidance from Your Angels Oracle Cards, Doreen Virtue, PhD

"Your task is not to seek for love, but merely to seek and find all the barriers within yourself that you have built against it." – Rumi, Persian poet and mystic (c. 1207 to 1273)

Love and the internal marriage of self is part of our own self-acceptance, part of fulfilling our peace and truest love. Deep within us, we are one, and to meet at this point, we marry our mind and body. In balance, trust, honesty, and love, we lose separation and become one.

Finding yourself is a journey that may take one lifetime – this lifetime or several lifetimes. There is no limit, and it is not a race. On the way, you will come across guides in the guise of your friends and family, each sharing and teaching you a little more about love. It is a mystical journey not shared with anyone. It is internal, and once experienced, it allows the wonderment of brilliance and of a beauty never sensed before. For this moment, you become one, and everything around and within you connects.

On finding and experiencing these moments of bliss, we can practice to revisit them anytime we wish, to rebalance and unite our mind and body. Through simple breathing, meditation wherever you feel comfortable, sitting quietly, yoga, walking, and swimming, it's your time and space to connect and "marry" you to simply be.

Marriage is far deeper than two people joining and committing to sharing their lifetime together. As this deepening love grows, so does our inner self with love and with no separation. A single traveller or with a partner, we all have the ability to experience the blissful place within ourselves, the place where we are one.

Today, tomorrow, and every day, we can return to our united self. be love. be light. be life. be happy. belifehappy.

Learning Happiness

. . . .

22 November 2010

"Happiness is a skill, a manner of being, but skills must be learned."
— Matthieu Ricard a Buddhist monk, author of *Happiness,*
A Guide to Developing Life's Most Important Skill

When we achieve major life achievements, we can feel a little disheartened afterwards. In these periods, some of us start to ask questions, and I certainly did. The first was what now. Where am I in terms of my growth? (This is very important to me.) With each step I take, I want it to be a movement towards my personal life goals of being happy and healthy. Then came the question of whether I was happy. I thought I was.

I have been blessed with being amongst two wonders of the world, the Grand Canyon and recently the Great Wall of China. I can share now that I was able to do this to the degree I was there on my own. There were people with me; however, I found space to experience the expanse of each of the places. Did I know what impact this would have on my life and of all the other natural and historical places I have been too and their beauty? No. And now I have an immense lasting appreciation of the fulfilment of these places. They, or more precisely, these experiences (not separate from myself) have created now an overwhelming sense of me, me being achievement of my goals and direction, fulfilment of my dreams, and the growing peace in my heart.

Did I understand what was happening? No, I didn't. Only recently with my realisation of what I really wanted from life, followed by a race and thirst for knowledge, here I am several years later, able to appreciate the daily work and practice of happiness.

I've always known I had happiness. I just didn't know, and no one showed me where to find it. It was inside me all this time. Happiness is within, and our greatest fear is to go within ourselves with our eyes wide open and see who we are, accepting who we are and loving who we are.

I let go of a world I hadn't been functioning very well in; I stopped as much negative noise as I could without completely cutting myself off; and I replaced it with happiness, laughter, and love. I chose to change from fighting every day to enjoying every day. I have found fulfilment within every book I have read and each new person and experience that has entered my life. My awareness has raised to the point where I would notice the brightness of this world, my world. I felt a love I had not felt before and a peace that brought so much joy. I would, and still do, smile a wide smile when I'm out walking.

I haven't been given happiness or just received it today. I practice happiness today, tomorrow, and every day. I practice what I was inspired to create: belifehappy.

When I bring suffering into my life, I know mindfully how to manage it. When my body becomes weak, I know where to seek the answers.

I am aware of me and of my life, and I love life because I love me.

Again, Matthieu Ricard wrote, "Happiness is an inner state of being," and whilst there are times when we lose faith in a moment of doubt, ultimately, we define happiness through our eyes and through our hearts.

Sailing on the Sea

22 November 2010

Now. Glorious sunshine with a beautiful winter breeze, and before my eyes is a picture view of the depths of the richest waters. With no anger or rage, the sea looks like it is filled with treasure with the beauty of a golden path reflecting from the sun. Here I am. And right now, I have it all, whatever the all is.

It's okay. My seat has a rusted car parked by the side, and out on the rocks was a fisherman blocking my view. It's okay because I have a new bench with a new view. It's okay because I will ignore the broken glass, cigarette butts, and plastic empty bottles surrounding my feet. Out there, right before my eyes, I can see what I am here for. The sea. The balance.

Over the last few days, my strength has been wilting, physically exhausted in a way I've experienced only once before. That's why I am here. I am here to remember how huge my world is and that I am my world. I have a choice of the view I wish to look at and see, a choice of what bench I will sit on, and a choice of what I can hear.

The sea and I have a meeting now to let go of the weaknesses and bring in some renewed energy, clearing my mind to identify what is on the board for 2011. We've got to really want what's here right before our eyes. Otherwise, how does it happen? I am here today to create my tomorrow. I am not creating anyone else's tomorrow. Just mine.

Through the golden yellow line on the horizon lives a vortex, a vortex for my thoughts. As I send each thought out through the waves, it is caught there in the vortex, and in return, I openly receive renewed energy.

We can all do this. Through choice, we can change any negative element of our life at any time we choose. If you were sailing a boat on this beautiful Mediterranean Sea, you are sailing east and decide in this moment you want to change direction and sail west. Would you turn the boat west? Would you choose to sail into the grey stormy clouds in the east or choose to the calm waters of the west?

We've all weathered storms and rough seas, and these are just tests and challenges to see and understand how far we have progressed and to experience if we are ready for what is next.

I'm not clear yet what is next. That's why I am here to see which direction I am sailing, and what I want to experience and create is an enjoyable journey.

I am blessed by this sunshine, the breeze, the sound of the sea, and this bench. Thank you.

Where are you sailing? Are your sails taking you towards or away from your desired destination? What would you do if you were steering this boat right now? Are you on course, or do you want to change direction?

Give: Value

. . . .

23 November 2010

Values are our interpretation of our world. They are internal and show how we place a value on ourselves and how we reflect these values externally. Simply, what value you place on something will not be the same as other people you come across in life. Therefore, we can find ourselves in situations where we feel disappointed that we didn't receive what we expected.

When we feel this disappointment, it can go unnoticed until one day it happens again and you just feel like you've had enough! Why are you not receiving what you feel is an equal exchange on the value you hold?

Overcoming this exchange requires us to look within and evaluate how we value ourselves in relevant and important areas of our life. This is a first step to accepting the situation. The next stage is to decide if you are willing to compromise your values to feel comfortable in these relevant situations. Or perhaps you will choose to leave the situation and move onwards.

Many people go through life feeling irritated, agitated, and even angry with others and particular events or situations and don't really knowing why they feel like they do. By establishing our values and beliefs, which we have formed from birth to now, we gain a greater insight as to who we are and why these things cause frustration. Identifying the root cause is half the work done. The imbalance caused by negative emotions builds up in our physical bodies, so finding that route cause will not only allow you to feel more relaxed and calm, but it will also ease your health.

The only question to ask is how you value your home, your partner, your work, your car, your clothes, your friends, your family, and your money. Absolutely – yes, money – all of these things. When you invest time in evaluating your values towards these major areas of your life and see what responses you have been receiving, would you want to change any areas? And what would happen if you placed a higher value on them?

What we value as important we will keep, look after, and treasure. What we place a lower value on, we may have no interest in or we may perceive that we lack this in our life. As you may have heard, there is no lack. We all have the ability to have what we set our mind and body towards achieving, believing, and receiving. If it's a low value, do you want whatever it is?

Give value to your life in a way you may not have seen before and be able to receive what you expected, release disappointment, and replace it with fulfilment and joy.

belifehappy.

Love: Your Driver

• •

25 November 2010

Inside the outer layer, there is a dark cave lit by a small fire torch. The man inside this cave is looking for a way out. He paces each day carrying his torch, asking when he will get to see more light. At the back of the cave is a stone bench, and the man resides himself there for hours upon hours after pacing. Here he asks why is this all I have? I wish I could have more light and find a way out. Is there a way out? He would ask.

Time passes, and the man feels no hope. He believes this is all he will ever have, this dark cave, the stone bench, and the one single fire torch. One day, the man was routinely pacing, and as he widened his space of where he was walking, he raised his torch and there before him were more pieces of wood. He could make a fire, and he would have more light. With more light, he could see his way out.

For many, this is life: inside a dark cave within ourselves searching for answers of why you don't have something. By focusing on 'lack of,' our vision will seek out what it is we lack and bring more 'lack of'. When we really know what it is we want to achieve, just by stepping out to the side, visiting a place we wouldn't usually go, we can become a step closer to where we want to be.

Let your purpose find you through a life you love.

Inside the cave is a victim and a driver. The driver found the wood and made a brighter fire to light up the whole cave. The victim sat on the stone bench not asking questions. He was still blaming the driver for bringing him into the cave. He was trapped in the angst of the past. He wanted to find a way out, but what if?

As the driver found a large stone that appeared with a white light seemingly pushing through, the driver pushed and pushed at the stone door. He called out to the victim and asked for help. He replied, "What's the point? We don't have the strength or tools to move that stone." The driver focused and focused, and he was adamant he would open this door. After several attempts, he stopped still on his feet, and there came flooding into the cave a beautiful light. As the driver's eyes refocused to the light, he smiled and walked outside.

The victim took slow steps towards the door. From what he could see, he thought, *What beautiful light, but what if I step outside?* The victim was afraid to leave the cave, and in the distance, he saw the driver dancing in the new light.

We are not required to be a driver or a victim – just to be ourselves. Each of us has both people inside a cave inside of us. It's our positive and our negative, our adventure and learning and our fear of the unknown. When they hold hands, they become balanced. We require the warnings of fear for when we are in situations where we might need to be in fight-or-flight mode; however; we require learning and confidence to experience life.

Through new experiences, we grow and become the people we are today. Positive and negative experiences both help us we grow. Love who you are and give thanks for who you are, knowing that every experience brought you to now. Anything you wish to change you can. You are a driver, too.

Christmas Joy

29 November 2010

Christmas brings a mixture of emotions, and managing them is a mindful task. Christmas is a celebration generally perceived to be spent with family and loved ones, where more than ever there are so many people who live away from their families.

Creating a Christmas that is special for you and those you share it with is the goal, and I also include those who choose to spend it on their own. We all have different expectations of Christmas, and through the removal of our judgment and replacing it with kindness and respect, we will have more energy to focus on our own holiday season.

Where worry and stress creep higher than the chimney, step away and take time for yourself. This is a time for cheer, and no one will enjoy it with the pressure that surrounds it. When you create calm inside yourself, you can share this calm within your home, too.

Life is balance – the balance of energy and of positives and negatives. To manage the balance manage your inner self through these mindful techniques:

Breathing

When you feel under pressure in the shopping queue, stop. Close your eyes for a second and smile inwardly or visualise a sunny day. Deeply inhale that feeling and exhale that feeling. By inhaling, you bring that feeling into yourself, and by exhaling, you share that feeling with those around you in the queue. Allow yourself to become centred and calm, and you will know this when you heart rate has slowed.

Planning

With Christmas nativities; school plays; and parties for the children, friends and family, there's lots more to do than in any other month. To prepare for this month, check all the dates and times and arrange your plans ahead of time. Have these in a place you will see every day. As the month progresses and other invitations arrive, at least you know what you have on already.

Smiling

Stuck in the Christmas shopping traffic, a Christmas joke on you – with any external stresses from situations or people, smile. Do it now, and notice how you feel. You instantly relax. Let go of any frustrations through your smile. We don't just have to smile with our mouth. We can also smile through our eyes and heart. Practice. When you smile through your eyes or heart, take your attention internally to these places and feel the feeling of a smile. You'll feel a peace within and know others can also see and feel it.

Awareness

Be aware of those you are spending time with. Everyone has some internal battle they are probably keeping to themselves. Kindness is the greatest gift you can give them. Whether you are a guest or the host, your kindness is contagious.

And my final tip is remember each moment to give, play, love, and learn. These will help you show kindness to smile, with compassion and love. Let go and accept. Feel lighter and freer as you enjoy each moment of this wonderful winter wonderland. The greatest gift is the gift of you.

A Bit of R and R

....

1 December 2010

There's still no snow here! Well, we're not expecting any. However, life on Facebook and Twitter would have me feel like I were. I am very blessed with some lovely friends who have been sending me photos of some beautiful snow covered forests in the UK though.

So whilst the chaos of snow continues in the UK, life here well, is here. Amongst the little challenges that have commenced my December, I've started walking before sunset each day to maintain my balance. The view is of immense light and power for the moment you look at the sun. All your worries and stresses of the day fall away, vanished in this natural beauty. I hope everyone here on the west coast gets to see this and feel it at least once a week.

Life continues, and with that continues the balancing act of mind and body. The sunset helps me relax both. I am aware that more people than me are experiencing the tightness of being here at the moment; I know it is no different in any other country, let alone the UK.

Wherever we make home is where we get to choose how to manage and respond to what life throws at us. I've learned so much, and whilst it's good to have a down day, it's great to start assessing what's happening, turning it around and just appreciating there is nothing you can do about it. If it is external, the only way to manage it is to let it be. When we attempt to control external situations, they actually use more of our energy, which we could be focusing on turning our view around. I have this wonderful home and internally peaceful life, and I've placed the do not disturb sign on it!

Each day brings a new brightness and a new love. I might not yet have achieved the balance I was working towards at the start of the week; however, through the challenges, I've been more creative. (I know my dad would be very proud of my cooking.) It's like I've been given the opportunity to use everything I have learned to date: accepting a situation, reviewing it, and knowing what action to take. So there you have it: a balance for mind and body. Nature and communication can help change your perspective!

To complete my day, I'm booked in with myself for a reiki session. Relax and reflect.

Love: Your Mistakes

. . . .

2 December 2010

Mistake. Mis-take. Without a dictionary, it looks like it was a "take" with a bit missed out. What a different way we can look at this word. What about the feeling of the word? What feeling does *mistake* create for you?

A take is like "take one" of your action play, and maybe we sometimes do "mis" part of the script, the scenery, and the emotions. On the stage, you have control, and you can change your script, the scenery, and the emotions anytime you choose.

Loving these mistakes is part of the play, part of life. Would we develop our lines to create more effect if we didn't have at least a few takes? Sometimes, it is just the rehearsal of a line that helps us test the reaction of ourselves and its effect on others. The mistake becomes a rehearsal, by which we can start to see that:

"There is no failure. Only feedback." – Robert Allen

Each mistake is feedback about your show. It's an opportunity to review and learn more about your response, actions, and emotions. Be constructive with your feedback of yourself: Would you say it like that to a friend?

With each mistake, know there is another opportunity that will present itself for you to have another take, this time for you to use your learnings. Whilst the mistakes are not usually enjoyable times and the learning can be painful, the satisfaction and fulfilment of experiencing new takes is awesome.

It's your chance to experience who you have become and how you have developed your talents.

No mistake is a failure. Rather, it is simply an opportunity for us to learn and turn our light up even brighter. Love your mistakes as you love yourself; they are part of who you have and will become. We all change. Everything changes. Some are big changes where the scenery moves, some are little changes in the script, and some are rewriting your script with new actors. This is your life, and as of today, we can all remove the negativity around mistakes because they are simply a mistake. So make your adjustments. They will improve your performance. Ready … action!

"No man is a failure who is enjoying life." – William Feather

The Road Stopped

. . . .

5 December 2010

What I've found this week is the road I was on just came to an end. No more a track. It's been left there for me to create and start building.

The only certain things in life are birth and death, and the bit in the middle is just a mess. It's what we make of the mess that dictates our outlook.

The mess in the middle has not been looking too brightly these last few weeks, and whilst I remain at best to retain my positive eyes, there have been a few occasions where it's looked quite bleak. Say you've been driving and then the road stops. Where do you go? And just like the road, I didn't create the dead end: It was given to me. With optimism in my heart, I decided to continue and take over building the road, except it's proving to be very challenging. There are no guarantees as to how each section will be completed.

There's a school of thought that would advise me now not to worry about the 'how' as long as I believe and act as though it is happening and be thankful when I receive it. It will all work out.

I think this works well when your road is built, and the only difficulty is you're lost and need directions. I can read a map, but the road is not built, so I'm finding it difficult to proceed to the next destination, without, of course, building each section of the road to get me there.

I'd not thought before like this because I took for granted that the road was and would always be there. When do we ever think it would just disappear? Left with no resources to build, we become resourceful and use the inner tools we have. There's no instant turn around. The work, through thought and focus, must first be in place.

I decided the best way to build my road was to be accepting and grateful for now, and when I say grateful, I mean for each breath, my health, the food I eat, my skills, and my friends.

There's no choice to not move or change, because movement and change is part of life. Without movement, it's like we have taken ourselves out of life. That's not an option. So back to building the road ahead, and I'm looking for green lights all the way!

Being grateful for each experience allows a greater self-awareness that allows us to share with others, contributing always to the flow.

Balancing the Peace Within

. . . .

6 December 2010

You know this week is a pretty big milestone week. I embarked on a journey to share a love and peace I had found in creating a life of happiness. What have I achieved so far?

As the journey started for me back in April 2008, two months after the sudden death of my dad, my life has changed very much, to a degree at times I don't think anyone in my life understands. After this event, not only did my hair begin going grey and curly, my inside wanted to change because if this was life, I wasn't living it. I went on and learned new skills, read a lot of books, and through family and people I met, I found and fell in love with me. As a result, I fell in love with life. Everything became brighter and more beautiful, and I really felt very happy inside.

It was difficult, too, as people who were in my life seemed to leave, and as soon as new people came, they also left. Everything happened so quickly, and I was learning so much. This year has been ultimately a year for me to experience and put into practice what I have learned. With this came more challenges. I suppose you could say I opted for physical, mental, emotional, and spiritual challenges. I'm still here!

Life has thrown me into a new place: one I've experienced before, just not to the degree of responsibility I now have. This too presents me with new fears I perhaps was not aware of (actually not admitting), and they are pretty big blocks in my life, so my next personal mission is to find a way of using my tools to push this big boulder (or two) out of my road.

What I guess I want to share is that I'm real. I'm Emma. I am at my happiest or ultimate joy when I am connected and feeling a peace that is very beautiful. However, I am earthbound. I live here, and I have to accept how the exchanges of life occur here. This is my new and next lesson that I've just started.

I created belifehappy because in my heart I am happiness. I have found peace and a love I never knew existed. However, this leads me to my next step in life, and for that I know I have to work hard to get there. That's part of the journey I chose.

So again, we don't find happiness one day and keep it. Happiness is a temporary emotion. Happiness for a lifetime is knowing and understanding how to maintain a balance in our lives through mind and body. And as life changes, as it does, we come across times when we need to adjust our balance to accommodate what we desire in our life. It becomes essential to make room, and sometimes, this means letting go or removing something already in our life. It might feel like a struggle, but through our eyes, we can always adjust the focus. Even when our bodies want to slow down, draw more energy into your body, breathe in more fresh air, smile more, laugh more, and share more. Through loving, we live.

Inside, I always have a secret smile that reminds me why I am here today and what I am doing. Love your secret smile, and know that you are truly amazing. Thank you for sharing your journey with me. belifehappy.

The Weather Outside is Frightful

11 December 2010

This is my favourite time of year, although the thing here is that you can't guarantee when the winds, rain, thunder, and lightening will start. This year, it's now.

I love this weather because it feels like it's doing something. There's texture to the skies, and the wind blows your hair and against your skin. The rain washes away the summer dust and winter sands, and everything looks fresh. Over the next month or so, the landscape changes, and the dry harshness of summer is replaced with an abundance of green richness covering our hills and coastline. The sound of the rain and the whispering of the winds makes me feel lovely and cosy at home. There's time to relax and snuggle.

It's not cold (well, for others, it's not); I seem to have wrapped up much earlier than most.

Someone mentioned the other day that there is no way I can be from England. I mean how would I cope with a UK winter, especially the one they are having this year?

There's another thing in the air here, too, which is not the weather: It's a festive spirit! Everyone wants to celebrate. So another Christmas Day is created! With the tree up and one very special friend who spent yesterday in the kitchen, I'll be celebrating my biggest Christmas with seventeen people for dinner. There's turkey and all the trimmings, and I spied with my little eye some beautifully homemade minced pies.

Rain or shine, the festive cheer is most definitely here.

Christmas is most definitely becoming different each and every year since 2008. The weather outside is frightful, and I know I feel delightful inside, because I have amazing friends all around the world and here right on my doorstep.

Are You Ready?

· ·

13 December 2010

I have found it difficult to write recently, and it felt like my tap had been turned off. In times like these, it's not a case of calling a plumber. Instead, it's best to just let it work itself through, and when it's ready and I am ready, it will come. Last night, the flow returned, and I was inspired by the blocks I'd experienced in the last few months.

I've been sidestepping committing to my goals for the coming year. I've not focused on them enough to create them. I've been focusing on only short-term goals and aligning myself to be ready to accept them. I needed to get ready.

For a few months, life was like jumping a hurdle and falling over, getting back up, jumping the next, and falling over again. I was running at everything to achieve my goals, and I can now look back and know I wasn't ready to achieve them. I know because now I am running towards the hurdle, and I feel like I am jumping over graciously and landing softly and continuing to the next. I am ready for each event, and I have learned how to approach, accept, and move through each event positively and successfully.

Is there a magic trick that helps us be ready? No. I can share with you that in my career, wealth, health, relationships, and domestic life, I have been falling at every hurdle, and I'm actually laughing and smiling to myself now. I wasn't in the last few weeks or months. I was tired, run down, and internally fighting with my world because it didn't look like how I thought it would. Then came the awakenings to show me what I was doing, and they were not too pleasant experiences. If they were nice events, we wouldn't notice, so instead we receive the mirror of what we ourselves are allowing to happen or not, whatever the case or lesson is. One after the other, they came galloping in. This time, my reactions were different from how I have reacted in the past. To an extent, I felt I was outside of me and watching this new person respond. The biggest difference was my assertiveness, and this is the card I received in an angel card reading I had done before all these events started to happen. At the time, I didn't know why I had the card! I'm not surprised I also got "listen."

In these last few months, I had managed to break at least three patterns of behaviour through what I had learned about myself. I was now using it. I was ready. The short-term goals I was reaching for suddenly were flowing towards me, to which each has been received with gratitude. So now I can look back and see the difference between the hurdles to reach my goals and now to them flowing, the difference between me not focusing clearly and letting fear dictate my direction instead of focus and confident intention.

I mentioned earlier that sometimes the best action is for us to get out of our way. We have this great ability to block the things we want in our life by not being ready to accept them. You see, that's what I have learned. When we ask, those things do line up ready for us, and when we are not ready for them, it's like we put up the red light. So when the things in your life you wanted to happen are not happening, ask what are you not ready for? Then ask why you are not ready for it and then ask what you are ready for.

Get out there today, and this week and be ready!

A Christmas Gift of Reflection

. . . .

20 December 2010

As this year nears to a close, with only eleven days until we reach 2011, the reflection of 2010 and aspirations for 2011 come more into focus. Personally, I'm feeling strength coming right through my feet, an amazing grounding, and with these stronger routes, I feel a great future.

Within my heart, I'm feeling stronger compassion and awareness of others, far greater than what I've experienced before. Life has placed card after card in this game, and whilst there are challenging moments, these are growing moments. Of this year, on observation, I feel it has been difficult for many to maintain a positive outlook.

I was asked how I felt about Christmas Day at the weekend, and my immediate reply was this: "I like everyday." I'm so very grateful to have this day and this moment now. What else can we ask for? We have air, and we can breathe. I do now have different feelings towards Christmas Day; however, they are memories, lasting lifetime memories of my last hug from my dad. I will be eternally grateful for that moment and the memory of it.

Recall a loving, happy memory and capture the whole feeling – the sounds and smells – because you can have this moment as many times as you want. Today, tomorrow, and every day. There are unlimited moments or as many as you wish to create. There are also unlimited moments of joy, love, and happiness for each of us every day; we just need to be aware of these, ask for them, and be willing to give and receive them.

"You're really crazy," someone said to me recently.

I replied, "No, just happy." I've talked about this before, that happy is a temporary experience. In that moment, I was happy. Why would I want to go out if I were unhappy? How would that make the people I'm with feel?

Our unhappiness is not going to improve unless we change something. No one thing or person can makes us happy. It's only temporary. Lasting happiness comes from inside us. Our feelings are contagious, so if you are sharing all your negativity, that's exactly what your friends, colleagues and family will be receiving and feeling from you. When you share your smile and positivity, that is what you are passing amongst your friends, colleagues and family. What do you want to be sharing?

So back to Christmas: What will bring you happiness on Christmas Day?

This week, find a moment of space in your mind to remember what you are thankful for this Christmas. It will truly light up your day amongst the external factors of weather, commuting, gift wrapping, and food shopping. This Christmas, fill your home with sparkles and smiles, laughter and love. If life feels a little bleak, please know that you are allowed to enjoy this season. Find those moments and thankful thoughts, and share them with those you love. Focus on changing and improving your situation, and simply by changing your perspective, you will feel better.

Christmas means what it means to you. Ensure it does mean what you want it to, so it brings you enjoyment to share with others.

Keep warm and safe, and I'm sending you all my dear love and peace. Remember happiness is for a lifetime, not just for Christmas.

belifehappy.

Fly Out of 2010

. . . .

28 December 2010

And fly I did. The scenery is a little different today and so is the temperature. Yes, here I am over in Blightly: home, mothership. Mothership is perhaps more my style and in theme with my flying.

As with many, many other expats, flying home for Christmas and New Year restores our festive spirit and is also a chance to check the radar on what it is like to return home. I, on the other hand, have returned as part of my return. It's a tough call when you live abroad to make the change again, but for me, this is becoming more of a pattern that I intend in 2011 to break (much to family and friends relief!)

We move abroad for our own reasons. We do the research we feel is right for us, and all decisions tend to come from the heart. As many people who know me will understand, I'm one of the few who actually likes change. Don't get me wrong: I do my best to commit to whatever I am doing, and when whatever I am doing is completed, I take a look around. That's when I make new plans, whatever and wherever they may be.

After returning from achieving an enormous life goal, trekking for five days on the Great Wall of China after having fundraised all year for the Mental Health Foundation, I became a little lost. Things also didn't appear to be working out. Signs were flashing, sirens were screaming, and I still wanted to push on. I sat and wrote some doodles for how I saw my 2011 and became very surprised at what was clearly on the paper before me.

Whilst I thought I had wanted these goals before, I had done everything to avoid achieving them. Now there is nothing else. I've experienced everything except for the goals I now have. Making and creating a life to allow these goals to happen was my next quiz question. After a lot of nudges, I finally woke up and said it. It was time to move on.

What was the alternative? I could stay and keep hitting my head against a brick wall?

Returning to the UK is not a glamorous or easy option. I'd done it before over three years, ago and it takes patience and a bit of settling back into. I have to say, though, that I've been out for my first trip to Tesco, meeting a fabulous friend there, walking back with the fresh air bursting in through my lungs, sat in the warm after having put a winter stew in the slow cooker, and had a warm cup of tea with a mince pie. I could and did have all this in my home in Cyprus, but this feels like home.

Every day is for following your heart. All your opportunities are waiting for you. Why wait for them? Create your dreams.

A New Year: What's Possible?

....

3 January 2011

There's a huge buzz of energy around this year, and the changes are happening now. It's incredible from a distance to then become aware of such greatness in mind. I've not watched television until last month, and the messages I am seeing and listening to are becoming more and more centred on giving, kindness, compassion, and joy. This gives us all a great start to 2011.

There's no escape! That smile you have today is contagious.

So while we can make a huge difference to how we feel, don't forget to keep in touch with what you feel. It is only a matter of time before we discover whether what we are doing is actually what we want. If we understand that what we do today is creating tomorrow, we will have control and happiness of our lives.

I'm personally starting this first week of 2011 knowing what it is I would like to achieve. The goals cover all major areas of my life and involve some travel around the UK, combining walking and visiting friends, as well as achieving another certificate. There are quite a few small goals, along with a couple of big ones. This makes for an exciting year ahead. What I've learned is that by creating these goals each year for the last three years now, I have successfully created a fulfilling life. I have achievements to celebrate that I didn't have before, and I have a direction I feel happy with and the flexibility for it to change.

When we believe in the impossible, the possible is created. (I'm possible.)

There is no one resolution for me as I've created a lifestyle that is continuous in development and balance, although I'm very ready to remove the excess mince pies, Christmas cake, and chocolate. Did I say mince pies? So my thoughts have been gearing me up to a running route, and I have my eye on a cross trainer.

Our thoughts set our direction, and with practice, each day, we can become aware of our thoughts and feelings. This is when our feelings will be our signal box to our direction. You'll know what goals are right for you and which aren't. Believe me, I know I will not shift the mince pies by replacing them with mixed berry pies. Maybe just mixed berries?

Allow your new year to be filled with health, wealth, and happiness.

Go easy on yourself, and remember that a happy mind equals a happy body. If you hear yourself using words like *have to*, *must*, and *should*, then rethink your goals. When you say your goals out loud, can you feel yourself smile?

Give: Time to be Thankful

. . . .

4 January 2011

After enjoying time sharing and exchanging gifts over the last week, more than ever, now is a great time to be thankful for everything in your life. Why now? A new year is like a new page for many of us, where we vow to stop something and do something. However, as you define a list of what you are thankful for, I wonder how many items you will find are not on your list and are still in your life.

What is really important to you this year? In fact, what is really important to you right now? Do you have it? Did it come gift wrapped? Or are you hoping it will happen or come to you?

A small thing overlooked is showing our gratitude, and by being thankful each day, what we don't realise is that this is helping us focus on what we do want in our life, bringing more of what we want into our life. How cool is that?

Worry, anxiety, and illness are all interrelated; we get run down by change and by circumstances. That's okay. However, what we want to help with is how to change this quickly and positively so you have your health. Everyone has a down day, and if you enjoy that down day because it gives you the excuse to have a well-deserved rest, ask what you could be thankful for and what would happen if you just let yourself have a deserved break because you enjoy it.

Through gratitude, we practice honesty with ourselves. To a degree, it's straight talking with our higher self. You're spending time investing in your thoughts and being thankful for them. Another way to look at this is to determine what will or did you appreciate in your day today. You could come home from the first day back in the office and be a little fed up that the fun festive break is over. Likewise, you could appreciate that you have a job. Focus on the good – the brightness of today – and give yourself a little pat on the back for being so amazing. You might not even know it, but perhaps a small act of kindness today (maybe you held open a door for someone or let someone in the car park have the space you were going to have) might have helped someone else.

This is all coming from being thankful. Being thankful in your thoughts really has so much power to transform your world and the world of others.

We all have a notepad somewhere in our homes, and we can all create time while cooking dinner or watching TV to write down what you are thankful for. You'll be amazed how amazing you and your life are. It's not a test. Everyone will have their own unique list of what they are grateful for in their life. And that is precisely the point: We don't live other people's lives. We live our own.

After the 500 words you just read, do you now feel just how powerful you and your thoughts really are? You can change anything, and sometimes without realising it, being thankful for what you love in your life brings you more of what you love in your life. Isn't that just the greatest gift? The instructions simply say practice daily. Go on, and be thankful.

belifehappy.

What Time Sent Me

. . . .

10 January 2011

Angels are never far from my side. I talk to them daily and every night before I go to sleep. I know that by keeping up this communication, they will remain close and help guide me, and last Friday, I felt this just when I needed it. I came over with the word *action,* and it inspired me to start creating a programme that I've started before and not completed, simply through other distractions and my own lack of belief in myself to complete it. I worked all afternoon and evening on this new programme and how it would help others and how I could get it to people. I was very excited. As I started researching before dinner, I looked at the clock, and it was 17:17 (number sequence of 717). Later that evening as I was finishing off my plan, the time caught my attention with 23:23 (number sequence of 323.)

Why would these numbers help me? According to Doreen Virtue's angelic number sequences found on the Spirit Library, the 717 at the start of my planning refers to:

"This is confirmation that you are doing great. You are on the right path, so keep going! This is a sign that you have chosen your thoughts well and that you should focus more steadily on your objectives. Be sure to add appropriate emotions to your thoughts; for instance, feeling grateful for the gifts you have in life. Gratitude will speed the process of your manifestations."

The 323 and the end of the plan refers to:

"The ascended masters are working with you as co-creators of your new project. They are telling you that they share your excitement and know that everything is working out well for you. The masters can see that your future is already guaranteed to be filled with the happiness you seek. Enjoy this new phase of your life!"

Whatever world you live in or I live in, isn't it helpful to know that secondary (in our world), there is a support system that is there to offer each of us guidance when we need it. We simply don't utilise this free resource as much as we could. Have you heard a story when someone has said, "I just knew... I was in danger," or "I heard something that made me turn back." Numerology is one set of signs we can use to be guided. I believe they use numbers with me because I sit at my Mac most of the day. It's the best way to get my attention.

With numbers and action, I feel a reassured progress in my world. The awareness and freedom in my mind is allowing me to create and enjoy each moment and work towards my goals. (I'm going to make that previous sentence one of my affirmations.)

One of the biggest mind fillers is worry, and we will worry about the past and the future and forget about the present. Letting go is a huge part of progression and action, and worry is often a way of avoiding or excusing our own progression through fear.

Free your mind to be now. Enjoy each moment knowing you are safe and protected, guided and loved, every step of the way. Today, tomorrow, and every day.

Anchor's Away

. . . .

7 February 2011

It's been a time where my world had a big shake up and clear out to start 2011 off with a renewed strength and vision. I wrote my goals at the end of last year, and as the last few weeks of 2010 came to a close, so came the realisation that what I wanted to achieve this year was not achievable where I was.

Any of us can remain in the same situation, wanting for a future we dream of. Then there are people who constantly create and open the doors to what it is they want to experience.

It's like wanting to go sailing and getting in the boat, but not releasing the anchor versus pulling up anchor and setting sail.

A question worth asking as we row steadily into the next year is to consider what, if anything, is weighing down your anchor? Our anchor is much the same and is what could be holding you back from realising one or all of your dreams.

For you visual readers, I'm going to ask you to visualise your own mooring. The water lapping towards the jetty. See the horizon and taste the salt air with each breath. Look now at your boat, and take a mental note of its condition. Is it luxurious and new, does it tell a story, and if so, what story? Or is your boat an old wooden sailing boat? How many oars do your have, or do you have a motor?

As you step onto your boat, take a seat and let the calm waves rock and soothe your mind and body. As you are ready to sail, ask:

Where am I going?
What do I want to see?
Is anyone traveling with you?
Whose journey is this?
Do you have everything you require for this trip?

Now start to pull on the rope to bring up the anchor.

How does it feel?
What does your anchor look like?
How heavy is it?
What could you let go of to release the anchor more smoothly to allow you to set sail towards your dream?

As you look forward out to sea (towards your next destination and goal) what does that feel like? Do you see your dream?

This year is about action, and to know we have achieved the results, we are required to review and assess where we are now and focus on where we are heading. The boat will go as fast or slow as you want. It's your journey; however, to set sail, we all are required to release what is no longer required. The journey is to the light, and to get there, we will become light(er). With this light, you will shine in your world. Others will join you until we all shine brightly, lighting together with luminous love.

We've entered a month of love. Light up your world as you release your anchor and set sail on your beautiful water.

belifehappy.

Life and Death

11 February 2011

Three years ago yesterday, I learned how life can change without warning. It was not only my life that changed that day, but I only know how it changed my life and my perspective.

The only certainty is change.

Life is a cycle, and you will have heard this quote at some time, I'm sure:

"We arrive in this life with nothing and leave with nothing."

There is always a beginning and end to every story, play, and movie. We accept that, and yet we are so surprised by death. We accept birth, so why is death something we literally shroud and keep quiet about?

I woke one morning and showered and dressed to have lunch with my family. I planned to meet friends for an afternoon drink in a local pub. By ten-thirty that morning, my day had changed. By eight minutes past eleven that night, my life had changed. It sounds very dramatic, and at the time, I did not know this was a life-changing moment. Three years on, I see what I have changed through my perspective and action to achieve the experiences I really wanted, not what I thought I should be experiencing.

Three years on, I have achieved and lived more than I had in the previous thirty-one years. I have given more, listened more, and loved more. After a childhood of confusion, teenage years of battle, and a fight for success and fitting in in my twenties, on this day three years ago, the events allowed me to see and feel the lack of living I was allowing in my life.

Accepting and holding the hand of my father as he died that evening gave me one of the greatest gifts in this life, and since that day, I have received many more. Why do we wait for our greatest fears to show us what we are not allowing? I secretly believe we don't wait. We just don't know what is really possible until we are faced with fear.

Am I afraid of dying? Yes, I think I am, only because I am young and have many things I still wish to experience. However, for me, the most liberating message from death is the gratitude I have for everyone and every moment in my life. I choose them all, and they choose me. I also work every day to achieve my goals – lifetime goals. I'm in no rush because I know my life is always progressing, and one day, like today, I will look back and see that progress. With joy.

It is not to live life in fear of death, but to live life because that is where you are right now. Just accepting that death is part of life allows us to release this daily fear.

In this lesson, I also learned compassion and the real meaning of love. Without both, I feel life is an empty cycle of commercialism and false expectation.

Our happiness is an individual measure of our own expectations and achievements. Our life is precious beyond means. The material, social, and status attachments are irrelevant. The only measure of success is our own, and the only measure of love is of the love we feel.

In a room with death, I became the person I feared I was.

I was sensitive, caring, and happy, and yet in this world, I felt this was wrong. Everything surrounding me telling me unhappiness was what everyone felt. That was wrong. My world has opened in unimaginable ways in the last three years by simply believing in how I feel: happy. To be brave and live life authentically.

Through nonjudgement and respect, we can build and bridge any gaps we have with loved ones in our lives. Acceptance is the key word. With no permanence in our life it is also a great lesson to learn that each negative situation is only temporary as we have all the tools within us to improve any situation.

The full stop doesn't need to be viewed as the end. It can also been seen as the beginning, the beginning of life now today, tomorrow, and every day.

give. play. love. learn. belifehappy.

A Different Passion

14 February 2011

Is your day filled with a deep love of you? Today, millions of people will be waiting for their loved ones and admirers to surprise them with how much they are loved. How wonderful! A day filled with love.

Love inspires passion, and today, I felt inspired to share a different passion, our inner passion for life. Passion drives us towards someone or something; it stirs action and enthusiasm. Does your love sound like this?

In a lost world, there is a lost passion.

For many years, I had no specific interest in anything. I knew what I liked to look at and experience, but passion was a strong word then, and I wasn't passionate about anything.

What ignited my passion(s) was life. In my lost world, I had many passions, and all of which I have now openly received. I gain so much pleasure from in my life.

Love and passion are very emotive, and we can easily overlook their importance in our life and within us. Love and passion are the soul and spirit of you. This is what we share with our loved ones. We share our love and passions for and in life.

Do you feel your passion? Have you lost it? Or do you not know what it is? We all have one. It might be our family, animals, charities, places, nature, architecture, history, or people – an endless list of passions that is so amazing because each of us holds our own unique passion(s).

We fall in love with ourselves and our passion, and others love us in return for our passion and love. How amazing!

Discovering and living our passions releases suppressed emotions and creates a freedom, and with your unique knowledge and experience, you have a gift to share with others: sharing your passion and igniting another person's flame!

This Valentine's Day, remember that love is deeper than the card you buy, the flowers you smell, the chocolate you taste, and the cupid's harp you hear playing in the background. Remember that the love and passion within you is more important than the love and passion you hold for others. What is within you, you share with others.

be love. be life. be happy.

Above and Below

. . . .

21 February 2011

It's all happening: electromagnetic surges effecting communications, a full moon over the weekend, and for me, lots of dreaming. As above, so below.

At the moment, I'm reading a couple of books by Mitch Albom. I was introduced to this author through a dear friend who bought the books for me as a gift. I've been surprised at how much I have enjoyed them, but my friend wasn't. She knew I would love them. Both books cover the approach to death and the people we meet in heaven. You might understand why I might not be that keen on the subject. However, what the books have done is provided me with a push and a thirst to ask a lot more questions.

With each question comes an answer, and it might come instantly, in a day or two, in months, or even longer. The part I have realised is that we will get the answer when we require and are ready for it. So these books have been doing both for me: answering questions I had and raising new questions that I look forward to learning more about.

One key question was: Am I already dead, and this is my life where I learn my lessons and make peace? Some of you will be nodding your heads, while others are thinking I've lost it completely! Seriously, we've all heard of illusions and energy and being connected all to source. There is an infinite source of where I am or where you are. What I am understanding is my own personal perception of the levels of life and the people in our life and understanding that we are not necessarily at the same stage. However, we are experiencing now together.

I'm beginning to understand and appreciate even more why I am here and what purpose I have above and below. Finding within has displayed the true illusion of my outer world. Only today I became aware that what I see outside the window is not the same as what someone else would see, and in fact, it is the same as what I would have seen more than five years ago.

Through this continuous learning, it becomes such a gift to appreciate, understand, accept, and learn from everyone and everything in this life. All of this, too, is creating a stronger foundation for me.

This leads me to ask: With the change I experienced a few years ago, am I now moving towards balancing my above and below? Am I now clearing the path at each stage, no longer storing old boxes of bad memories or emotions and opening the door to kindness and love?

As you start your week, work through this day, stopping for a second to think about how others may see a situation. Watch how and where you feel your emotions and how you can change them, become more aware of you, and notice how small positive actions create and open the door to kindness and love.

The angels wait for you to ask them to share their love and light into our world.

We ask and accept the angels' love and light into our world.

Change

· ·

28 February 2011

We are at the end of another month, and this week starts the brand new month of March. I'm creating my own mantra for this month: "I march with a spring in my step." March is a frantically fun month, don't you think? We associate January with new beginnings, but in March, for many, we see the colour bursting back into our gardens, the air warmer, the smell of hot cross buns in the bakeries, and the taste of summer not far away.

This change isn't what most of us feel comfortable with because it really does change our life. It is said we cannot appreciate the light until we have experienced the darkness, and what I find and have learned is that by embracing, accepting, and learning in the dark, the passage to the light is within my control. I own the change (the light switch).

Feelings of discomfort and frustration with our life is often simply a symptom of change. And by recognising (awareness) and allowing changes to flow through our daily life, the symptoms disappear and the change becomes constant. We benefit from positive movement in our life.

Our ego stands in the way of many changes and is often the reason we stay within our safety zone. When we are in a positive balance, we challenge our ego and always get great results.

My 2011 started with a brand new location, surrounded with my family and dear friends. It also meant I left other dear friends; however, they remain close in my heart. This is one of the pains of change that we accept – our material world and relationships will be affected. However, with positive change, the people who love and support you will continue to. Those who are on the sidelines will move on and watch another game, and new supporters will join you.

Have faith in the wonderful power of love for yourself and how it manifests your life surrounding you. Use the resources of family and new friends to help you on your journey, and always know each person who enters your life is there for a reason. Enjoy the experience!

A Walk with Nature

. . . .

21 March 2011

There's something about nature I forget when I'm going about each day. Every morning, I sit and eat my breakfast and drink my cup of tea watching the birds swooping into the garden and settling for a moment of one of the bird feeders or the water bath. I watch the different birds who come to visit, some with amazing colours, but all oblivious to what a friend said last week to me:

"A great day for the race."
I replied, "What race?" (Are you are there before me?)
"The Human Race!" he replied.

I've mentioned previously about daycations. This really struck me when I was listening to the radio in my car coming home from work. Daycations are vital to our well-being, and to this, I agreed and realised that I've not been allowing this time into my own life. No more timely than a Friday, as this meant I could now plan my weekend to ensure I did something different.

It can feel like nothing much and therefore not worth the effort to get in the car or take a walk. I, like many of you reading, have chores to do at the weekends (I've not found the ironing fairies, – although I keep looking!). I do balance some of the washing during the end of the week, so the ironing is all I have at the weekend (still on today's to-do list, in fact). However, whatever the chores for the weekend, I really knew just how important it was for me to have some time out. I packed a light rucksack with my camera and headed to our local woods. This was not only for a walk in nature; I was also joining a Distant Healing session held by a dear friend.

As soon as I pulled up and parked, I instantly noticed the freshness and calmness the towering trees offered. With my first steps into the woods I noticed small white feathers on the path. I just knew I was not alone. If anything, the feathers helped me relax as I started my short trek around the woods.

I have quite a few questions, and it was nature reminding me that I already had the answers. I'd just forgotten the basics of how nature reflects our human world. As I was breathing in the oxygen of the trees, the trees breathed in my carbon dioxide. Is there a simpler example of the balance of nature? I wish I had listened more in my science classes, but thankfully, it is never too late to learn.

We all have many different beliefs, and some people may not really be aware of what they believe in. The thing is to leave judgment aside. Where I am coming from, to explain this walk in nature, is a mirror effect. We might not like what we see, and we can close our eyes for as long as we like. However, what we don't want to see will still be there until we accept it. I walked along a smooth pathway and found a bench where I'd sat before I took another path. This one was a muddy dirt track with lumps and bumps, where walking required a skilled dance to get to the end. I think that reflects my life pretty well right now!

Then I heard, "You can't see the wood for the trees." This was a message I received a few years back, and I guess it just came back to me. This time, however, as I was patient, just looking ahead, I began to see there was a pathway through. It might not have looked like it from where I was sitting, but it was there.

And there was the message: "However muddled events can appear, there is always a path to guide you through. Only with patience will it appear."

In my daycation, I felt balanced and grounded, received and sent healing, and reminded myself of some very important and very simple natural lessons.

I ask you to notice nature. It is here for a reason, and once it becomes part of your life, today, tomorrow, and every day, it supports and guides us in ways we ignored before. What is nature reflecting in your life? (Don't be surprised to see lots of beauty and immense light – because you are!)

Changes are Even Quicker

· ·

28 March 2011

The end of March and four years ago I sat and wrote about finding happiness. Now I'm here with a cup of tea, some chocolate, and a mountain of ironing. That's reality, isn't it?

How I prepare for this mountain is all about my attitude towards it and what I feel I will have accomplished when it is complete.

March has been, for many on an individual level, a month of action with some turbulence. What comes next? I don't have the answers to the future; however, guidance from the now, which we all have, reminds us of our appreciation and gratitude for our life, living from a place of love daily. This alone will help, sending waves of love and healing (again, we all can do this) and restoring balance on a greater, universal level.

Time is perceived as flying, and by that I mean rapid changes and back to an individual level. Change will become more frequent, and with it, please enjoy the changes. Many a hurdle may need jumping, and when you reach the end of the track, you will feel immense elation.

It's also a growing time for me, and I am the only person responsible for creating this time, and this coming month feels right. When I started 2011, I had some major goals, and whilst some of those got ticked off quickly, others I started to doubt in March. After becoming aware of my doubts, I changed my thoughts. I can say more ticks!

In those times of reflection like I am approaching, I already see a pattern of changes emerging in my life, and it shows me that as of the end of each month of this year to date, I have experienced many wonderful gifts and surprises.

It's all down to keeping the faith and the belief that you deserve what you wish to achieve and keeping the belief right in the forefront of each day. Know and believe in its manifestation. Your dreams do come true. The times they don't come true is when we change our mind and decide we don't want it anymore. Right now, I feel infinite love and gratitude for everyone I am blessed to have in my life and for my health. With all those amazing people in our lives (write them down now) and our health, we have the power to succeed in all areas of our life and help others achieve their dreams, too.

Clearing Way for What is Waiting for Us

· ·

4 July 2011

Seriously, if there is one thing I can put my hand on my heart and say is that your kitchen cupboards are a true reflection of your life. Now as I work with honesty, I can share with you now that I don't have any kitchen cupboards. When I did, they were pretty empty, which was a complete reflection of where I was in my life at the time. Now, I share three kitchens, and there are three spare rooms all with my name assigned to them. I see that as growth!

Back to you and your kitchen cupboards. I often hear people say, "go on Emma tell me what that is in that fairy world of yours." The simple thing is whether fairies or angels exist (which I am 100% sure they do!), you are your life. What you have placed in your cupboards is you.

Now look at what is in them. How they are placed, is there ease of reach, and what is that jar of pickles in the back corner? Thought that got finished off? Like so much in life, it got pushed to the back of the cupboard. This might be a familiar thought: "if I leave it there maybe someone else will throw it away and deal with it?"

It would be great if the above were true. When do you start to take responsibility for your life? Who is cleaning or repacking your cupboards?

On an inner level, everyone is managing their own life, so by depending on others to do it for you, you will unfortunately (if you were waiting) see it will never happen. This is not to say you are on your own. You are not. There are always people around you who are waiting to step in, help you reach the top cupboard, and start to sort through the out of dates and things from the past that now can, with your acceptance, be placed in the bin.

Where you see darkness in those cupboards, a close friend will see light and share the it with you. You continue to make decisions about the food in there and whether it is food you want to have now. Where it isn't, be okay with it and let it go.

Food shopping and food consumption are all part of this process. The cupboard is simply where we store (in the short, medium, or long term.) The flow and respect for the flow will have an effect on whether things in your life tend to go off. Quite simply, when you are buying what you want and are supportive of who you are (that includes your family and house guests), the food will flow healthily and clearly. That too is life. When we think and invite healthy, clear, and supportive thoughts into our life, it, too, flows freely – without clutter.

Be supportive of your life. Check your cupboards to see what you are storing from the past.

The Myth of Change

· ·

21 July 2011

Change is easy. It is a myth that change is difficult. The decision to create change is simple. You've made it! What is difficult is learning the process that comes with change. The truth hurts, and whilst I don't promote hurt, I'd like to say that the truth comes along and reflects right at us in every situation – positively and negatively – as we move through change.

You've created the change in thought, you agree with the change, you have aligned your values, and your beliefs for change, so you're ready. Yet at certain stages of manifestation of the change, we become faced with challenging mirrors that reflect a learning to help us grow. To an extent, they test us in whether we really want the change we have asked and agreed to.

By learning self-awareness by expanding our senses or our inner guidance system, we can trust the reflections. We can stand back and ask, "is this in alignment with where I am now?" Being truthful and honest is another way to assist with change.

Change affects us physically and mentally, usually with the mental driving the physical (unless you are focusing on health and fitness; your physical body might then drive the mental change.) Your awareness of your physical body is paramount to accepting the change. In situations where you see the reflection of the past, your physical response will communicate with your mind. The key here is to ensure your physical body is properly nurtured during transitional changes and that it is creating positive and aligned responses.

You are your best advisor. You have all the answers you are willing to see, listen for, and accept. When you feel sadness through change, honestly ask what the reason is for your sadness. Your answer will be a reflection of the past. Then ask whether this is supportive of where you are now and where you want to be. It's okay to be sad. In fact, it is okay to feel whatever you feel. With self-awareness, however, you can allow a core source of guidance to provide you with the truth, and when it hurts, learn, accept, and focus on you and where you are now.

You are amazing, so allow yourself to share this. Fighting change is simply fighting yourself.

Love the change, and love yourself.

be love. be life. be happy. belifehappy.

To Find out Now

. . . .

March 2012

The train journey

After living thirty-four years of nothingness, I was now in what feels like no man's land. I'm here, and I can see, feel, and hear, except there is a feeling of certain unsettledness in my world. My head begins to feel fuzzy, and I notice that actually it was less than 24 hours earlier when I had discovered what I actually believed about myself. Goodness! What had I done to myself over all those years!

I ask a lot of questions. I'm a pretty curious person, always knowing there is something for us to learn in every moment and situation. I even – of no surprise to many – ask questions of myself (well, we do hold all our own answers), and I now find myself asking how was I living when I placed no value on myself and believed myself to be empty and nothing.

Was living with nothing living? I have thirty-four years of life. It is necessary to make sense of this life as it was or more importantly learn as I now embark on a new life. Sounds pretty huge? It isn't.

I'm still on my way home, which is currently where I hang my hat. It has been a long journey from Cornwall, and I'm starting to really notice my life and the immensity of changing nothing into completeness. Can you see that?

I wonder now if the question you are asking is, "how did I discover I believed I was nothing?" (Actually, what did that feel like for me?) Well, when we are faced with emptiness, ultimately, the only direction is completeness.

Five years later, the journey to find happiness is complete. The rest of this journey to be continued as life.

PART FOUR

365 Inspiring Messages

1. Give. Play. Love. Learn. Today. Tomorrow. Everyday

2. Be you. be life. be happy.

3. Working hard to achieve your goals is part of the experience. If it was easy we would not learn on our way.

4. Learn from everything around you. You learn so much from a friends' experiences and knowledge. Ask questions. Your friends are your teachers.

5. Structure in life is a great thing. Even greater is the ability to change and challenge the structure. You are the creator of your day.

6. The light shines brightly each day. Only you control the brightness. If it is dark, change the bulb. If it is dim TURN IT UP!

7. Be the love that shines so brightly, be the love that holds you tightly, be the love. give the love. YOU are LOVE.

8. With love you reach a step higher within yourself.

9. Love and light fluttering your way for a relaxing end to your beautiful day. belifehappy.

10. Light up your senses towards love and awaken your love of YOU. today. tomorrow. everyday.

11. Give time. Give kindness. Give love. Today turn UP your light and brighten someone's day.

12. AwesomeNess sparkles fluttering your way to bring extra love into your day! You're AmaZING.

13. Create play in your day. today. tomorrow. everyday. be inspired. be creative. be joy. be life. be happy.

14. Listen to your body. Rest or get active. Give to yourself and share with others in your life.

15. Anything which gives you joy is giving you time to love yourself.

16. Be the light of greatness in your day. be great. be light. be love. be life. be happy.

17. We have a world full of creatively inspired playtime, and we can find joy in everything we do. Look at your world and ask how can I play today?

18. From within give your SMILES to your world.

19. Tonight, rest your mind and body in the darkness and know you always shine as brightly as a star.

20. Fill your life with kindness, give, play, love and learn. belifehappy. today. tomorrow. everyday.

21. The greatest gift of this day is... YOU. Wear a smile and share a smile.

22. Welcomeness to this beautiful morning... breathe in this new day and exhale yesterday!

23. What is the most outstanding moment in your day today? Not got one? Create one NOW!

24. Stretch up and reach the sky. Take out a smile from your wardrobe and be the sunshine in your day! Let's GO!

25. Allowing peace in your heart allows peace in all areas of your life. To find peace. Simply. be you. be love. be life. be happy.

26. Turn every moment of tension into a smile. For the moment of the smile is NOW and the tension becomes past. Let go.

27. It's FREE!.... Kindness. Give it. Accept it and SHARE it.

28. This morning brings a brand new sky, which opens up for you to fly, high and bright throughout the day, for you to enjoy and embrace YOUR day.

29. Look for the gifts your life presents you with each day. Accept them with love. be love. be life. be happy.

30. Be balance. be health. be peace. be joy. be love. be life. be happy.

31. Love. It is always within you. light. kindness. gratitude. joy. Peace.

32. Each person who believes in helping others is making a difference. Collectively we are helping.

33. Welcomeness to YOUR wonderful day! A simple action of a positive thought plus a smile.. and you've just made someone's day!

34. Be rested. be joyful. be smiles. be love. be life. be happy.

35. You know the feeling - excited, bubbly, with smiles? Are you feeling it NOW? Go on! Flick the switch and smile W I D E.

36. Morning sparkles fluttering your way to brighten your path and help you CREATE your day.

37. Turning the darkness into light, changing any moment of unhappiness with a moment to remember lightness and be thankful.

38. Enjoy a limitless day by allowing yourself to make a choice.

39. There is no secret except for what you have not found within you... yet.

40. A day filled with light is a day filled with happiness, as love, joy, peace and harmony are drawn into your day.

41. Believe in you. Only you have the power to place limits in your life.

42. Be relaxed. be peaceful. be balance. be love. be life. be happy. This moment. Now.

43. A spark of the unconscious brightens the dreams and creates action. Who creates your inspired spark?

44. A simple word 'change' is our key to life. Add 'constant' before and see your tree blossom.

45. With the sunshine in your heart you will have brightness and warmth around you. today. tomorrow. everyday.

46. Allow your day to be a reflection of you - AMAZING!

47. Be the love that shines so brightly, be the love that holds you tightly, be the love. give the love. YOU are LOVE.

48. Be peace. be restful. be relaxed. breathe slowly. breathe deeply. be sleepy.

49. Give yourself time to be aware of who you are. That is LOVE. A simple step to loving you. today. tomorrow. everyday.

50. Simplicity is the best form of love we can give ourselves.

51. Z.I.N.G zone in now GO!

52. MorningNess sparkles fluttering your way to wake you UP and be ready for the most awesomeness of days.

53. Love and laughter sparkles and shine - you, yourself are the divine. Go shine and light up the world today.

54. Releasing fear, releases the locks on all your doors. be free. be true. be you. be life. be happy.

55. With love you reach a step higher within yourself.

56. Any weaknesses you have right now will always be overcome by your passion. be passion. be you. be life. be happy.

57. Give yourself time to be aware of who you are. That is LOVE. A simple step to loving you. today. tomorrow. everyday.

58. Do something each minute of each day that takes you towards your milestones and dreams, and you will find happiness. be love. be you. be life. be happy.

59. The cycle of giving and receiving is eternal. Give joy and receive joy. Give love and receive love. Keep the cycle moving.

60. Breathe in peace and restful skies. Let go of all your worries and say goodbye. Sleep well.

61. Your hands are amazing. Give a helping hand today.

62. Don't be surprised by your talents. We always knew they were there.

63. When you stop living a life of others fears, you will dance through the change. be change. be living. be you.

64. Step into your light and stand in your LOVE.

65. We do not have to wait for someone to love us before we are able to love ourselves.

66. When you focus your energy on what you really are passionate about, you are in alignment.

67. Love is a sea within me. The flow of energy. The balance. The universe.

68. Who is the love whispering in my ear? Who is the love cleansing me? Who is the love inspiring me? YOU. You are the LOVE.

69. Start your day by shaking off yesterday. From top to toe shake your arms, hands, body, legs and feet.. Then take a deep breath in...... breathe in a whole new day... and breathe out yesterday.

70. Be your love. be your change. be your life. be your happiness. belifehappy.

71. Have an awesome day filled with fun and laughter and thank you for being you.
72. Confidence only comes from belief. You believing in YOU.
73. When we stop fearing, we start learning.
74. To be in the flow, in alignment and in balance helps us review, appreciate, be grateful and move onwards brighter and happier.
75. Let the night sky show you how bright you truly shine. today. tomorrow. everyday.
76. Give: you today. Share who you are with others and remember you are a gift.
77. Do not fight things of today. Ask for help. Accept help. Give help and glide through your day.
78. The doors are right in front of you. Keep your focus and they will open wide.
79. When we allow the time to play we bring back the power of learning into our lives.
80. Let's turn UP the brightness in your day and play. today. tomorrow. everyday.
81. Love: the ultimate of healing is love. be love. be life. be happy.
82. When you tune into love, the words lead the way.
83. Love is where you meet me. At the place inside where the rivers stop their divide. The water flows as one.
84. Be joy. be laughter. be kind. be you. be love. be life. be happy.
85. Learning is a balance of positive changes and releasing the negative past. Enjoy learning. today. tomorrow. everyday.
86. Now. I AM Love and I AM loved. be thankful for the love. today. tomorrow. everyday.
87. Life becomes love and loving becomes living. be love. be life. be happy.
88. With focus you find your love is inside of you all a long. Not hiding, just a little help with igniting.
89. With play you light up your mind and body so that every cell sings and dances. be play. be joy. be light. be love. be life. be happy.

90. Let love be your gift to you, to share with others and, to give to those who do, share your light, your smiles, and knowledge, let your love learn, and be your life college.

91. be honest with yourself. be.

92. Just feel it..... you know it's there... warmth.. it's starting... a smile... :-) relax.. breath.. the love.

93. Start today with a smile and carry it with you all day and feel the sunshine shine brighter.

94. Many teachers and many minds. It will only be your thoughts which create your time.

95. The changing time of the changing moon, Will come through and all too soon, You will feel the choices abound, For only you can surround, yourself with riches, abundance and love, You are only, You are love.

96. A bank balance does not indicate success or failure. Your heart is the richest asset you own.

97. Choose happiness today. tomorrow. everyday.

98. Can you feel it? Then take three deep breaths, stretch up to the sky then stand and affirm: I am love ten times. Wishing you all a day filled with love.

99. In times of uncertainty call upon love. I see love. I hear love. I feel love. Love is around me. Love is within me. I am love. Now feel how safe and protected you are.

100. Be joy. be inspired. be creative. be seeing. be feeling. be hearing. be love. be life. be happy.

101. Sparkly sunshine fluttering your way to bring beautiful light to fill your day!

102. Affirmation give: When I give to others I give to myself. be giving. be receiving. be balanced.

103. Give: a smile: see the joy. hear the laughter. feel the love.

104. The universe is all. You are the universe. You are responsible for your universe and its balance.

105. Giving is part of the balance cycle and in effect we can choose to ignore it.. until the imbalance gets your attention.

106. Give thanks to your 'champions' the friends who are not always there day to day, all the time they are championing you, believing in you and sending you love!

107. As long as you remain a believer in you, your path will illuminate and shine. The obstacles are there for us to learn and grow.

108. Think about today. Enjoy. today. tomorrow. everyday.

109. With love and respect our world is abundant in opportunity, a free flow of joyful communication - down to a simple SMILE.

110. Affirmation: I give love and thanks and I am open to all opportunities.

111. Recipe for today: Start with adding a smile. Jump up and down and mix with laughter. Add joy and calm. Be still for two minutes. Then sprinkle all over with love. Have an AWESOME day. (Add HUGS)

112. Confidence comes from happiness within. Happiness within comes from joy and love of what you are doing.

113. Through lost eyes the world is sad. Through living eyes the world becomes life. be living. be love. be life. be happy.

114. Love is inside of you, a candle light glowing and growing with love. You are surrounded by lots of candles and you all shine brightly together.

115. Play is a free flow of joy, there is no uneasy feeling, instead you welcome achievement, excitement, confidence, and relaxation.

116. Create play in your day by releasing your full potential.

117. Affirmation: I have an abundance of time in my day to achieve..... (fill in)_____

118. When you control time, you are in time. When time controls you, you are out of time.

119. Fall in love with your internal world and share this love with the universe!

120. In this moment release negative expectations in your mind and watch how life flows beautifully.

121. Everywhere, with open eyes, I learn.

122. The universe of which we are all collectively part of is awesomely amazing... to feel it, see it and hear it.. we just have to listen to ourselves.
123. Love of yourself is the most unbreakable love there is. With this love all external love flows.
124. On our own we individually glow, together we shine.
125. Your ego said "time is running out" and your higher self said "you have NOW" be now. be love. be life. be happy.
126. The greatness of your heart will always be rewarded. Your kindness ROCKS!
127. I believe in my purpose and my purpose motivates me. I believe in me and my purpose is me. I motivate me and therefore I must be two parts to make ONE 'I' and 'Me' becomes 'We'. We are part of ONE. The purpose? LOVE.
128. Love is transparent, unconditional and clear, it offers itself for free for all your years. You are love.
129. Love is invisible unless you OPEN your eyes and accept it. Give and receive love. today. tomorrow. everyday.
130. Clear your mind, rest your body, give love, play love, learn love. Love is the source. Embrace its warmth. today. tomorrow. everyday.
131. Love yourself and become free flowing and relaxed, check your pace and balance, look out for warning signs and give thanks each day.
132. No expectations or time exists except for the expectations and time you limit yourself with. Enjoy your moments.
133. You ARE your light, a stunning, awesome, shinning beacon of joy. We LOVE you.
134. Get that ZING! in your step today - discover your ZING. Zone. In. Now. Go!
135. Joy is an unconditional emotion, filling us with happiness, by experiencing new activities of play in our day we will create more of these brief moments of unconditional joy.

136. You become your light, a stunning, awesome, shinning beacon of joy. Do you feel it? Are you seeing is right NOW?
137. As ONE we are simply, I AM.
138. The 'attitude of gratitude' allows free flowing experiences in your life, moment by moment.
139. By being thankful you accept experiences. I AM receiving and I AM grateful to receive. I AM in control of these experiences, and my direction of thought will direct the outcomes.
140. With laughter and smiles, love and cheer! Hip Hip Hooray! You are here!
141. Finding your uniqueness to the world is like finding your treasure and when it comes the sun shines brighter than ever before.
142. We are responsible for what we create in our day. What experiences are you creating today?
143. You are an entertainer! What experience do you want to create for your audience?
144. When you are running around for tomorrow you're not focusing on how special today is.
145. Today is beautiful. Tomorrow too. Everyday is beautiful.... with you.
146. Turn OFF the thinking and START being YOU! Yay! First answer, first feeling.. Let's Go!
147. The moment of beauty, peace, love and joy you have been looking for.. You can have it right NOW. be still.
148. Start your day refreshed... breathe in deeply, fill your body... and let... go. Let your week go. Today is a brand new shiny day.
149. Sunshine sparkles fluttering your way, Hip Hip Hooray!
150. Find give, play, love and learn in love. Love is your gift which you allow for yourself. Stay open to love and let its frequency flow through you. today. tomorrow. everyday.
151. Falling in love with ourselves is the searching and meeting of who we really are and being truthful with what we believe, see and feel and be our true purpose. Sometimes we have to let go of the past to allow you to be you. You are LOVE.

152. Love: This morning when you are dressed and look in the mirror, see only love surrounding you. Breath in love and let it fill your body and exhale...letting go... letting go... inhale more love.... and let go. You are LOVE.

153. Let play carry through your day with music to lift your soul and move your feet.

154. Play lifts us and makes us lighter. Let go of the tension of today and find different ways to play.

155. Start your day with play! Do something different.... have a different cereal, hug everyone in your home before you leave the house, change the radio station in the car, and SMILE at everyone at work! When someone asks what's wrong with you.. tell them you're having a belifehappy day!

156. STOP: STAR ALERT! Step in your light NOW. TURN IT UP! Let's GO!

157. Enjoy giving effortlessly from your heart with love allowing you to grow your love of your life. today. tomorrow. everyday.

158. When we act out and live through our hearts, our mental and physical bodies are aligned, giving us health.

159. Why do we get surprised and upset when what we asked for or thought about actually happens! Think about what you do want and let it flow.

160. This is your lifetime of happiness, through your choices, acceptance and love. What choices will you make today to create a day filled with happiness?

161. Happiness = being honest with yourself.

162. Tip for the day: Smile from your heart. Your warmth will radiate through you and around you. Share your love through a smile.

163. Find the child inside of you; play, listen and learn.

164. It's not magic - it's focus, dedication and passion that leads people to live their dreams.

165. Love: the moment you are in. Feel and see the light within you and watch how everything around brightens. You light up YOUR day!

166. When you woke up this morning you had a choice. Consciously choose to have a GREAT day filled with smiles and laughter.

167. The power of our breathing lends much to our inner calm and peace.

168. Play: from the heart and share your FUN with EVERYONE!

169. Play: stone, paper, scissors. We often forget to play childhood games. be fun. be creative. be laughter. be play. be life. be happy.

170. When you cross the river you may slip on a stone, get held back by the flow, but eventually, you will make it across the water (if you want to!)

171. Repeating messages and events (positive and negative) are great guides to our inner happiness.

172. Each day is an opportunity to take steps towards your dream. What will you do today?

173. Be thankful for the day you have had. be thankful for those you care for. be thankful for love. be love. be life. be happy.

174. Experience living from your heart and watch your dreams unfold. You are your dreams. be love. be life. be happy.

175. Be kind to yourself, it's a great place to start and share your sparkles with others.

176. We all dream and they become reality when we allow ourselves to open our eyes and see our dream. What do you choose to look at? Are they your dreams?

177. Today is a day for play! Start your day with a smile and follow with laughter! Have a FUNtabulous day!

178. Give: your dreams the reality they desire by focusing your intention on what you would like in your life, (not what you DON'T want).

179. The love. My love. Me. Flows. Endlessly. To you.

180. Focus Pocus! Let your intention be, all for what and only you see, and wish to be.

181. Welcome with love all that is your day, and as you close your eyes give your day to the starry skies.

182. Follow your heart and it will lead you to a place where your dreams are.
183. Open your internal wings and fly as you were intended to. We are all angels. be kind. be love. be life. be happy.
184. When one light stops shining in your world, it has only moved higher to shine brighter and illuminate your path with love. be love.
185. Be kind. be laughter. be light. be love. be life. be happy.
186. Be thankful of people and events in your life right now. Learn from them. Through this process you are able to release and move clearly in to your next moment. Create a day of learning and releasing through your day.
187. In the looking mirror of love is your reflection. What do you feel and where do you feel those feelings from your reflection? Send into your looking mirror thoughts of peace, kindness, joy, light and love. be love.
188. Have you invested in your creativity bank? A bank that supports your dreams.
189. When you have reached the point where you know and practice everyday control and ownership of your time.. you will be able to be, do and have anything you set yourself to achieve.
190. Believe in yourself - and watch and feel how your random kindness starts to create changes in your life and in the lives of around you.
191. Your light shines wherever you are. We follow, share and feel the joy and peace radiating from your light. We are light.
192. Affirmation: I am trusting with each day and moment I am working towards my goals.
193. It takes only ourselves to travel and firstly choose to travel, remembering there is no destination, just stops on the way, with the idea to accept, learn and let go of what you see in the rear view mirror, and then keep on driving forward.

194. As you start your day check your internal balance switches 1) switch them all to ON 2) push the levers UP.. Turn UP the brightness in YOUR life! Have funtastical fun.

195. Why do we call someone we don't know a strange (r) - for it is often people we don't know who offer us the most love and support on our journey.

196. Through our own desire for happiness today. tomorrow. everyday we can practice to connect to our love from within, and the more we connect the more we see it reflected in our daily actions, words, and choices.

197. This new love is one to embrace and share, it offers acts of kindness and supports us all on our journey, providing more ease and less disease, more love and less fighting. be love.

198. Have you thought about whether you are in love with yourself? There is a definitive shift occurring where love comes from within and then lights up our world.

199. Are we conditioned to not play as we get older? Play it loud, sing it loud, laugh loud!

200. How bright is the sun, the moon and the stars, They are only as bright as the eyes that are, aware of their light and of their love, Are you aware of the world above?

201. Awareness of our world brings awareness within and the beauty just keeps flowing.

202. Imagine your body today as a calm glistening lake in the sunshine, where everything moves and everything changes effortlessly. Breathe through the ripples of the water, relax and float. be love.

203. Tip: go barefoot and feel the grass tickle your toes or your feet sink into the sand. For a few moments focus on this connection. Enjoy and have an awesomely fabulous day.

204. We enter this lifetime with a contract for the house we moved into.

205. Let your home be your protection, maintain it, love it and share it's wisdom, skills and knowledge with kindness. today. tomorrow. everyday.

206. Play inspires and promotes our creativity. Play with love.

207. It takes one person one word or action to inspire and motivate another. You can motivate and be motivated. be inspired. be action.

208. Hip Hip Hooray! Today is TODAY! With lots of sparkles of happiness fluttering your way to inspire play in your day! Let's GO!

209. Throw yourself into today, take the name of the day away and simply enjoy each moment.

210. Close this day with love. be peace. be love. be life. be happy.

211. Live for your purpose and your true beliefs and when you feel a hesitation just ask why?

212. Our inner changes are in response to our higher self guiding us to be who you are in your true light, with your true purpose. A life where you do not feel in battle, a life where your talent, skill, knowledge and kindness shine and radiate.

213. Take a step forward today, create a space and time to be still and allow yourself to feel calm, safe and loved. You are loved.

214. The break of a new day is an opportunity to break old patterns. Start the day with a smile and watch what a difference you will create.

215. Be thankful for right now. Be relaxed and feel calm, for now is still today and what you feel right now will be remembered today. tomorrow. everyday.

216. With no action we create no change. What are you doing today?

217. We can spend our lifetime hiding, excusing and fearing the truth and not living our full potential.

218. Love: is YOU.

219. Each day without fear, a little bit more of your potential world reveals itself. One step at a time.

220. Trust in yourself and which way you are going. First Ask. Second Listen. Third Be. be love. be life. be happy.

221. There is nothing more exhilarating than doing something you've not done in a while. Experience again how good it makes you feel. Play.

222. With today's renamed 'twoday' you also get the idea of balance.. of two.. mind and body, giving and receiving. Think today about your balance. You might be giving, however do you allow yourself to receive? And is your body telling you anything which could help your mind? These few minutes of daily awareness will make a big difference.

223. Many of us limit our feelings because of the 'day' it is. What would happen if today was Tuesday and not Monday... How would you feel? Your thoughts when you woke up today and in this present moment create your day... What are you creating for today? Go be and do awesome things! Let's GO!

224. Just for this one moment... stop... and remember... just... how.. amaZING! you are.

225. The mirror on the bathroom wall reflects what you choose to see. Emotions form in our physical body, so what emotions do you see? be honest. be love. be life. be happy.

226. You hear what you think.. Start today by telling yourself how beautiful you are, relaxed and ready to enjoy the days ahead.

227. Find two minutes to close your eyes. Breathe and see, feel, hear and think about how you would like your weekend to be. Create it now. Set your intention now. Open your eyes and we wish you an awesomely fun filled weekend.

228. Allowing and reminding ourselves of our inner love, our life source, creates more balance and happiness. be love. be life. be happy.

229. Love delivers ease in our life.

230. Start your day with the look of love. For a moment stand and close your eyes, draw your intention to your heart and imagine

white light filling your body and surrounding you. OPEN your eyes. BRIGHT! SHINE! Let's GO!

231. Be playful. be joy. be creative. be inspired. be you. be life. be happy.

232. The only person stopping your dreams from coming true is ... you. What could you do today to start being your dream?

233. Give: thanks.

234. Our words are not a barrier alone... our thoughts are too. be open. be light. be love. be life. be happy.

235. A box stored under your bed on top of the wardrobe or under the stairs represents a box stored in your mind. Process, learn and love the memories. You can keep the box, you just don't have to carry it with you.

236. Learning something new or making a change can be difficult and you'll feel like giving up. Take a moment to look at what you are bringing into your life (and to others around you) to what you had. Does it feel better? If the answer is yes then be thankful and let go of what you had, release it and enjoy NOW!

237. We have nothing to fear except ourselves. We create a limits, and we can also remove them.

238. You are a reflection of all the beauty around you. Focus your senses of the greatness of now in your life. be beauty. be love. be life. be happy.

239. Let the light shine throughout your day, through all the people you share laughter, love and play. Shine.

240. Love: our jobs are labelled with a title, and in some cases we are labelled. Today you will take a new label; GIFT! You are a gift to this life. be love. be life. be happy.

241. Everything in your life presents an opportunity to give and receive. Keeping the balance is the key.

242. Nothing more than you, because YOU are amazing and YOU are Love. be amazing. be love. be life. be happy.

243. Dancing feet always worn by smiling eyes.

244. Where you are right now is a reflection of the thoughts you created. What are you thinking NOW? Act as if you are.

245. When we begin to understand that people and events come into our lives for a reason, to share with or to learn from, we feel more in flow and are more thankful for these experiences.

246. It's not magic - it's focus, dedication and passion that leads people to live their dreams.

247. Love: the moment you are in. Feel and see the light within you and watch how everything around brightens. You Light YOUR day!

248. Love is knowing you are love, loved and loving. be love. be life. be happy.

249. Be. Let go of the past. Be. Seeing the future you desire. Be. NOW. EnJOY.

250. To follow our heart takes courage. Like the lion in the *Wizard of Oz* our heart grows and becomes fearless. be love. be life. be happy.

251. One of the greatest gifts is to allow ourselves to feel life. be life. be happy.

252. Allow yourself to let life carry you. There are no wrong turns, just experiences to grow from, providing us with strength through giving, playing, loving and learning. belifehappy.

253. When we give way to fear, we give away opportunities. be fearless!

254. Whether the weather distorts the clarity of your vision, don't let it distort the clarity of your thoughts. Be clear and focused with your intentions for this day and watch how the negativity floats away, allowing you to enJOY the most successful day! Let's GO!

255. Hip Hip Hurray it's time to play, feel love and laughter in your heart throughout this wonderful day!

256. No one outside of you can 'pay you back' for any wrongs you've felt. Only you can punish yourself or make peace. Your peace is always inside of you. be peace. be love. be life. be happy.

257. Love + love = love. You can't subtract or divide love, only add. be love. be life. be happy.

258. Give with love and intention to continue in the flow of life. The size or action of the gift is irrelevant, it really is the thought which will be received.

259. We have this great ability to block the things we want in our life by not being ready to accept them. Are you ready? Get ready... GO!

260. What your mind is thinking your body is feeling, your eyes are seeing and your ears are hearing. You CAN change what your thinking to feel, see and hear a brighter picture! Turn it UP! Let's Go!

261. Allowing our adult self to have fun takes time. Let your inner child take over and see how much FUN, laughter, love and play comes your way.

262. In forGIVEness we receive love.

263. Give: compassion and kindness from your heart. be kind. be love. be life. be happy.

264. Be YOU. be love. be life. be happy.

265. No mistake is a failure, it's simply an opportunity for us to learn and turn up our light even brighter. Love your mistakes as you love yourself.

266. As you get ready to start your day, think of you and say: I am warm and loved inside and out, from head to toe, I am ready for today so now, let's get on with the show.

267. Looking after our immediate environment has a BIG effect on how we feel. Take time for yourself and your home to create YOUR peace.

268. Today is bright, today is clear, release and let go of fear, today is now so fill it up with lots of cheer! Happy Morning! Let's GO!

269. A smile from the heart shines through the eyes. Light UP your today and those around you.

270. Happiness is within and our greatest fear is to go within ourselves with our eyes WIDE open and see who we are.

271. Love and the internal marriage of self, is part of our own self acceptance.

272. Love is the answer see, today is simple, just let it be. Now.

273. Play: let the sound of life carry you your way, choose the music to set the pace or your day.

274. Slow down and enjoy life. You have everything inside you NOW to enJOY today. tomorrow. everyday.

275. Today turn to a new page in your story. Create, learn and experience this fabulous day. Let's learn.

276. In peace we travel. In life we love. be peace. be love. be life. be happy.

277. Through eyes of love, we feel joy.

278. Create a moment of simplicity. Think, see and feel love. NOW.

279. With no excuses, your world becomes limitless with opportunities to play.

280. Complete your day with love and ask for help, support and guidance, because someone is always listening.

281. The only alignment a belief needs is to be aligned with the person asking to receive.

282. Letting go of what was is the only way to enJOY what is.

283. Love is what guides us. It comes as light. You are radiant light. Thank you for brightening our world.

284. Are your steps leading you towards or away from your dreams?

285. Your world is never waiting, it is always within you.

286. Your mind becomes free and awareness becomes focused on a different view, from inside. Love inside out.

287. Peace within draws a light, With each visit day or night, The light simmers, flickers and grows, Until over the days, months and years, we know, The light takes flight reaching far and wide, Reaching up to the skies, invisible of course to the human eye, This light becomes a floating mist, soothing like a kiss, Touching each of our human souls, Protecting each step, and guiding us with love, to our goals.

288. What we can never be sure of is being sure because you can only 'be' right now.
289. Joy will be in each day when we all open our hearts and let our light guide us, inspiring our dreams.
290. Welcome to this amazing moment. A moment you created. Create all your moments today from love.
291. Feed the stars your worries and concerns before you sleep tonight. They are waiting to shine brightly and guide you along a peaceful and joyful path. Be rested.
292. We succeed by being only ourselves.
293. Fall in love learning and accepting who you are. You are amazing inside and out! be love. be life. be happy.
294. Choose kindness from your wardrobe this morning and wear it brightly throughout your day. Shine brighter.
295. Be your hero. today. tomorrow. everyday.
296. With closed eyes you can often see more. When things get cloudy, stop for a minute. Close your eyes. Breathe. Then open your eyes wide and see what you couldn't see before. Have an awesome day!
297. Love: breathing for clarity. Allow your breathing to give you the vision of calm helping you make the right choices for you.
298. There is enough time to do something different.
299. Right now.. just remind yourself how amaZING you are. You are love, light and you shine brightly. Thank you :-)
300. BELIEF in yourself is enough to achieve anything you wish to achieve. Learn from others, and respect each others dreams.
301. No matter how we feel, there is always a moment to feel love.
302. Live and enjoy the gift of our senses, be aware of the beauty that is within us and around us in every moment.
303. You have a gift to balance your awareness with feeling the greatness of who you are and where you are and the people who are with you now.
304. Thoughtfulness is a currency underestimated.

305. Turn down the noise and give yourself a quiet perspective of now.

306. Whatever the weather, wherever you are, the forecast today says you are a STAR. The sky will shine brightly from each of our hearts!

307. Simplicity guides life. Assumptions lead us to judgement and judgement creates limitations. be simple. be light. be love. be life. be happy.

308. Love: listens. be love. be life. be happy :-)

309. A true friend is like a looking mirror with your faults and perfections, with the answers and truth of your unconscious, which speaks with only love.

310. Happiness is an individual measure.

311. Being YOU is where the real JOY is. Being who you think other people would like you to be is not real and therefore not joy.

312. It's always there, always within us. Each gift is simply part of YOU.

313. I want to share this love, for each of you today. I want to share laughter, in each moment we play. I want to hear the music, in each word you say. I want to feel your smiles always, everyday. I want to share the magic, to dance this life with you. I want to light each day with the light of you. I want to breathe the air I share with you. I am the light and the love that is you. I am. We.

314. Right now we can't change anything external which might be happening tomorrow (AKA worry). What we can do is choose to think thoughts which support us, keep us focused, and smile. Because that smile - your smile, will lift your heart and the hearts around you.

315. Monday mornings equal magical moments :-) Create yours today. tomorrow. everyday.

316. Find the switch. Turn it on. Turn it up. Happiness. It's in YOUR control. today. tomorrow. everyday.

317. When you believe in you, the world does too. Don't wait for the world, as the world is you x

318. When we fully align ourself with what be believe - this is our reality.

319. See, feel and hear the power in these words: I AM ALIVE.

320. Give someone space and they will find a way to fill it, some will temporarily fill it, others will accept the space and trust it has been created for a reason.

321. I am worthy, I am value in the world, I add value in the world, I am the world, the world is you, me, we.

322. It's totally OK to be who you be now? Lovely, now for a cup that cheers! (tea).

323. Change.. a bit like a snow blizzard, it's hard to see everything, you feel a bit out of control, and inside you know with care and intention you'll make it through.

324. I can live with contrast and know it is there to show me what it is I don't want and what I am grateful for.

325. Your authentic light shines brighter for longer. Have you found the right light bulb and switch?

326. When I follow my heart the truth whispers love.

327. I can fill any silence with love, I can fill any fear with music, I can be.

328. Mirror, Mirror do you see? I feel the fog surrounding me, I ask my mind to push me through, It tells me "No, only you.", Inside my head I look and see, the fog will lift, when I choose me. I choose me!" I cry, With that I bid the fog goodbye. Bid goodbye to depression.

329. It's totally OK for you to think, be and do who and what you want to be today, as long as it is OK with you? be you. be life. be happy.

330. Good morning sunshine smiles. What could you do to create a magically amazing day? Yep that's it.... You know!

331. A fiction book character can be perceived in as many ways as there are readers. YOUR mind creates the story and the movie.

332. Write down ALL the things you love. How many are you doing and being today? be YOU. be love. be life. be happy.

333. Consider each day you give a little, play a little, love (lots) and learn a little... how amazing would each day be? today. tomorrow. everyday. give. play. love. learn.

334. Taking a rest is often the least thing we think we have time for when we are up against things. Rest brings clarity. Now do you have time to take a rest?

335. Listen... to the words and much more than words which are spoken. A message for you, a lesson for you, listen to the stillness, listen to the breeze, listen for the unspoken words sent with love.

336. Your success is not down to whether other people believe in you. It is all down to whether you believe in you. be YOU. be love. be life. be happy.

337. Give yourself space to honour your emotions, to learn lessons and to love, so you can play. give. play. love. learn and belifehappy.

338. The real challenge to change is in resistance to change, how willing are you to let go to learn and grow through life's presenting changes?

339. Holding back happiness? Letting go and accepting love in your life is like drawing back the curtains, flinging open those windows and feeling the breeze flow and the sun shine effortlessly. be love. be life. be happy.

340. A great gift in love is trust and acceptance in what is, not what was or what maybe, simply love now. be love. be life. be happy.

341. We don't need to explain our love. We only need to show it.

342. Hiding the truth is like hiding your happiness. be your truth today. tomorrow. everyday.

343. Give Love. Play in Love. Be Love. Learn from Love. today. tomorrow. everyday and belifehappy.

344. I am grateful for each moment. I am joy in this moment. I am happiness. today tomorrow everyday. I AM. Love.

345. Good Morning smiles. Your happiness is within you. From head to toe you can choose to smile and share your smiles today. tomorrow. everyday.

346. Give thought to your words and actions today. tomorrow. everyday.

347. Is it really an option to not smile today? It's all down to you. Just remember your smile brightens your day.

348. Here's something for today, remember the magic. And I say Yay! for magic! Have an awesome day.

349. Be in a place of mind-full-ness. The alternative is mind-less. Act with purpose and intention. be mindful. be life. be happy :-)

350. Your intention for helping others will provide your outcomes.

351. Life shares millions of blessings - you are one of them.

352. Feel empowered today. Step into YOU, your light and your love, reminding yourself of every wonderful aspect in your life. Shine brighter than ever. today. tomorrow. everyday.

353. Go easy on yourself, change becomes more frequent when we accept it and allow all the greatness to flow into our lives.

354. Open your day with intention and close it with love and gratitude.

355. Burst with colour. today tomorrow. everyday.

356. Give yourself the life you want. If you want chaos and drama then this is what you will see. However if you want calm and beauty then this is too what you will see.

357. Everyday consciously take a mental and physical step towards your dream. be your dream. be. be life. be happy.

358. Given there is a delay between your thoughts and manifestation, would the time to write down your thoughts, creating them exactly as you wish, be an amazing investment? Journalling helps us focus our thoughts, direct them towards where we want to be, and use it to see how our patterns have changed over time. You'll be amazed when you invest time in you.

359. Affirmation: I feel infinite love and gratitude for everyone I am blessed to have in my life and for my health.

360. Be YOU. That's all anyone ever wants.

361. Life resembles a series of stepping stones we choose to reach a defined goal or our life purpose. Take each step with light, joy and love :-)

362. There are no if's, buts, maybe's, should, must, or could have's. There is only now. today. tomorrow. everyday. belifehappy.

363. When your world is calm, you can see, feel and hear your dreams. Find calm in your day.

364. No more. No less. Be always your best. today. tomorrow. everyday and belifehappy.

365. When is the right time? Now. be now. be life. be happy.

Epilogue

26 March 2014

It's seven years since I began my quest to find happiness, and in one month I will be walking down the aisle. Would I have found this lifetime love without the love I found in me? This was my big goal, the one I'd been avoiding. I'd been choosing empty cupboards, but for how long could I do that for? I knew what I wanted and my return to the UK helped me find just that.

I would not be who I am today without the experience of depression, the loss of my dad or the healing journey. My husband would not have looked twice at who I was seven years ago. To be honest neither would I! I wasn't who I wanted to be. I learned a new way of life and love and that is how I found my lifetime of happiness.

I met my husband in the summer of 2012, a few months after accepting and welcoming completeness in my life. We're both very thankful too my grandmother saw us engaged before she passed away. It felt a little like she was waiting to see me settled, and to have found happiness and the unconditional love she had shown me that day in her flat.

Everything around me seems to have grown; I have more family for starters and it feels wonderful. I am very grateful for this whole journey; creating belifehappy, learning and being belifehappy and sharing belifehappy with you. Thank you.

What next?

The journey continues with give, play, love, and learning to be life happy today, tomorrow, and every day. Each day is for following your heart. All your opportunities are waiting for you. Why wait for them? be you. be love. be life. be happy.

give. play. love. learn. belifehappy.

With love x

About the Mental Health Foundation

. . . .

The Mental Health Foundation is the UK's leading mental health research, policy, and service improvement charity. Since 1949, it has worked to improve the lives of people affected by mental health problems, reduce the suffering caused by mental ill health, and help everyone lead mentally healthier lives. This is achieved by:

- Carrying out groundbreaking research and evaluation
- Developing practical solutions for better mental health services
- Campaigning to reduce stigma and discrimination
- Promoting better mental health for everyone

It works across all age ranges and all aspects of mental health. It is the charity for the nation's mental well-being.

Its work incorporates the Foundation for People with Learning Disabilities, a leading national organisation working to improve the lives of people with learning disabilities. It is widely recognised in the learning disabilities sector for its ability to deliver innovative projects making a real difference. In addition, the Children and Young People's Programme is dedicated to working with and understanding the issues that are important to this especially vulnerable group.

For more information, please visit www.mentalhealth.org.uk
Tel: 020 7803 1121
Email: info@mentalhealth.org.uk

Mental Health Foundation
Colechurch House
1 London Bridge Walk
London
SE1 2SX

About the Author

Emma is the founder of belifehappy. She is a trained NLP and hypnotherapist practitioner and coach, reiki master practitioner, and holistic massage therapist. Additionally, she has a 2:1 BA (Hons) degree in business studies and a postgraduate diploma in marketing. Having lived in Cyprus while writing *belifehappy*, Emma now lives in her hometown of Market Deeping, Lincolnshire, with her husband.

Lightning Source UK Ltd.
Milton Keynes UK
UKOW06f0958070315

247453UK00001B/31/P